IN GOOD COMPANY

IN GOOD COMPANY

❖

*How Social Capital Makes
Organizations Work*

Don Cohen
Laurence Prusak

HARVARD BUSINESS SCHOOL PRESS
BOSTON, MASSACHUSETTS

Library of Congress Cataloging-in-Publication Data
Cohen, Don, 1946–
In good company : how social capital makes organizations work /
Don Cohen, Laurence Prusak.
p. cm.
Includes bibliographical references and index.
ISBN 0-87584-913-X
1. Organizational behavior. 2. Corporate culture. 3. Quality of
work life. I. Prusak, Laurence. II. Title
HD58.7 .C6214 2001
302.3'5--dc21   00-059739

The paper used in this publication meets the requirements of the
American National Standard for Permanence of Paper for
Publications and Documents in Libraries and Archives Z39.48–1992.

To Helen, Rebecca, and Sarah;
Brenda, Kim, and Ben

Contents

Preface and
Acknowledgments

Most of us know from experience that trusted colleagues help us to accomplish our work. We know that we respond differently and better to respect than to ridicule. Most of us know that the experience of working in isolation for any length of time can be lonely and dispiriting. We know too that we are more likely to give our energy, talent, and loyalty to an organization if those around us are helpful and honest as opposed to uncooperative and devious, and if the leadership of the organization takes a fair and equitable approach to the people who work for it. We know we do better work if we have a chance to get to know our coworkers rather than continually adjust to a changing roster of team members. Most of us would rather do good work than merely go through the motions in order to collect a paycheck. When we have lunch with colleagues or spend an hour in a hotel or airport lounge with them during a business trip, we usually talk about work: we wrestle with a stubborn problem together, describe an unusually successful (or disastrous) work experience, or exchange information on what has been going on elsewhere in the organization or the industry.

Oddly enough, this common experience—these obvious truths, we would say—tends to be forgotten when people talk about organizations. We know we do not enjoy spending weeks isolated from colleagues, but commentators tells us that telecommuting will grow and grow, with millions of workers happily home alone with their computers. We depend on gradually developed ties of trust and understanding with colleagues, but the organizations of the future (we are told) will consist of free agents who meet briefly to carry out a particular task and then move on to some other temporary configuration. Whether we are doctors, salespeople, help desk experts, or researchers, we learn from "shoptalk" with our peers, but many organizations act as if the time we spend with our coworkers in the lunchroom is wasted, a way of avoiding our "real" work.

To put this contrast in general terms, we experience work as a human, social activity that engages the same social needs and responses as the other parts of our lives: the need for connection and cooperation, support and trust, a sense of belonging, fairness, and recognition. But analysts still often see organizations as machines (for producing goods, services, or knowledge) or as an assemblage of self-focused individuals—free agents or "companies of one"—who somehow manage to coordinate their individual aims long enough to accomplish a task. As much as anything else, this disconnection between how people experience organizations and how experts describe them has prompted us to write *In Good Company*. Related claims that new technology is utterly transforming society—that much of the work of the future will be "virtual" work—have also spurred us to take a look at the persistent social realities of organizations that balance and often refute those claims.

Our subject is social capital in organizations, the trust-based connections between people, and the networks and communities through which they engage in cooperative action. Social capital is not a new subject, but most analysis has focused on individuals or nations, cultures or regions, rather than on organizations, and much of this analysis is quite abstract. In this book, we offer a practical and down-to-earth approach that demonstrates the nature and value of social capital in organizations and suggests how leaders can invest in this vital source of organizational strength.

To a considerable extent, the "feel" of an organization (or "the smell of the place," in the words of Sumantra Ghoshal and Christopher Bartlett) tells you whether it has high or low social capital.[1] Anyone who has visited organizations knows how quickly the experience of wandering around creates an impression of a place. The way people greet (or ignore) each other in hallways, the look of offices, comments overheard in elevators or elicited by questions, the emotional atmosphere (energetic, disheartened, angry, optimistic, bright, grim, friendly, suspicious), among dozens of other signals can answer—often very accurately—the question "What kind of place is this?" The answer to that question matters. Visitors to the old British Leyland parts subsidiary, called the "worst factory in Europe," found grim, suspicious workers and grimy, outdated factories. Visitors to Unipart, its newer successful incarnation, see the "sparkle" in workers' eyes as well as immaculate and well-equipped facilities.[2] The feel of the place heartens workers, improves work, and attracts customers. A recognition of the importance of all these factors leads executive search firm recruiters trying to fill a critical position to look beyond resumes and letters of recommendation and ask people they respect in the industry, "What is she really like when you get to know her?"

We try to capture the feel of organizations in this book, to remind ourselves and our readers what they are "really like" as opposed to what a flowchart, mission statement, or theory says they are like, because social capital resides in that reality. In part, we rely much more extensively on our own and others' experience of organizations than on models and statistics, because the subject of organizational social capital is too new to have generated much evidence of that kind. More importantly, though, our focus reflects the fact that social capital resides in the daily life of organizations. A largely descriptive, experiential approach is appropriate to the subject. We tell stories because stories communicate the complex social realities of people and organizations.

Because we believe in the lasting importance of social capital, we expect those models and measures to evolve as the conversation continues. They can have great value, provided their roots are nourished by the reality of organizational life. Our own approach is not entirely impressionistic and anecdotal, though both authors place a great deal of stock in impressions and anecdotes. We also look at some of the "harder" evidence of social capital in organizations such as retention and longevity rates, social network analyses, and employee-satisfaction survey results.

In the interest of developing a reasonably clear, organized approach to this complex subject, we have to some extent divided it into component parts that have no independent existence in the real world. Our topics—including trust, networks, communication, and participation—are closely intertwined. We hope that our dissection does not murder the living entity we explore here; we have tried to keep the entire social organism in view even as we considered one or another aspect of it. When we fail to do that, we count on our readers to put our remarks in the context of the wider subject and their own experience.

Acknowledgments

Not surprisingly, we could not have written this book about connection and collaboration without the help of many writers, friends, and colleagues. We cannot possibly mention all those who have enriched and improved our thinking through their writing and conversation. We would like especially to thank Paul Adler, Chris Bartlett, John Seely Brown, Sarah Cohen, Rob Cross (IKM), Rob Cross (SAS Institute), Tom Davenport, Sally Dudley, Liam Fahey, Jerry Frank, Joseph Horvath, Linda Kalver, Jim Keane, Bruce Kogut, Peter Lawrence, Eric Lesser, Dan McMackin, David Mundell, Chris Newell, Kim Prusak, Barbara Saidel, Chuck Sieloff, Rick Stone, Etienne Wenger, and Michael Woolcock—an important few among the many who shared ideas with us at meetings, during phone conversations, and over meals. Experiencing the intellectual generosity of others has been one of the pleasures of working on this project.

We also want to express our great appreciation to Steve Denning, Nitin Nohria, and Bob Sutton, whose extensive and thoughtful comments on our first draft made this a better book than it otherwise would have been. Our editor, Hollis Heimbouch, supported us with incisive comments about how to improve our manuscript and especially with her enthusiasm for the subject and our approach to it.

We also owe a debt of gratitude to the careful and intelligent editorial attention of Melinda Adams Merino, Amanda Gardner, and Genoveva Llosa of Harvard Business School Press.

It is customary for authors to thank family members for putting up with their fatigue, distraction, discouragement, and crankiness while struggling to complete their book. Fair enough; we are grateful for that forbearance. But we would also like to express appreciation to Helen, Rebecca, and Sarah, and to Brenda, Kim, and Ben, for their encouragement and their active demonstration of what trust and relationship mean.

IN GOOD COMPANY

1

❖

IN GOOD COMPANY

No man is an island, entire of itself;
every man is a piece of the continent, a part of the main.
—JOHN DONNE

ASK WHAT COMES TO MIND when they hear the name "UPS" and most people will mention those chocolate brown delivery vans. They are everywhere in the United States, part of the landscape of its cities and towns, and their brown-uniformed drivers are a familiar presence at homes and offices. The effects of service reductions caused by a Teamsters strike in 1997 showed how enmeshed United Parcel Service had become in the daily commercial life of the country.

Talk to people inside the company—drivers, managers, executives—and many will give you remarkably consistent explanations of what it means to be a "UPSer."[1] They mention long-term commitment and hard work in a "no-nonsense, roll up your sleeves" kind of company where everyone pitches in to get the job done regardless of what their primary responsibilities are. The stories they tell echo one another: of veteran drivers instructing neophytes about how to keep winter winds out of the "package cars" (as the delivery vans are known internally) or where the farmers on a rural delivery route gather on a rainy day; of the eight-months-pregnant center manager who took over the route of a driver who called in sick, and the national customer service manager who helped load packages during the Christmas rush ("getting his hands dirty like the rest of us"); of the company founder, who personally answered every customer phone call. They talk about the people who have been with the company for thirty years or more who have "brown blood" in their veins, of former mentors, now retired, who still call to see how their protégés are doing.

Beginning as a small messenger-carrying service in Seattle, Washington, almost 100 years ago, the company soon expanded into package delivery for local retailers. Its territory now includes every address in the United States. It delivers by air as well as ground, internationally as well as nationally. In 1999, when UPS publicly traded a small proportion of its stock for the first time, it had about 300,000 employees and was widely seen as an integral part of the new world of Internet commerce. Through almost a century of growth and change—and think of the enormous technological and social change that has occurred between the pre–World War I years and the beginning of the new millennium—the company has maintained a surprisingly consistent "feel." Change continues. As an article in *Forbes* magazine naming United Parcel Service its company of the year for 2000 stated, "UPS used to be a trucking company with technology. Now it's a technology company with trucks."[2] But the values and behaviors that characterized the firm from its inception persist, and current UPSers still regularly cite the ideas and actions of founder Jim Casey to explain what they do now.

People inside UPS attribute its lasting success to elements of its persistent "character." A low turnover rate—around 2 percent for managers—makes long careers typical and helps preserve and transmit the firm's values and behaviors. Along with creating a shared understanding of how UPS works and what its aims are, longevity gives people extensive, diverse experience in the company and well-established networks of relationships. A tradition of promotion from within means that leaders have direct experience with the work of drivers and their supervisors. (Well over 90 percent of those attending the annual meetings of the company's top 200 managers have been with UPS for more than twenty years.) That promotion policy, good salaries for drivers, and employee ownership (with company stock available to anyone who has worked at UPS for thirty days) contribute to a sense of equity in opportunity and reward and joint membership in a common endeavor.

UPS's culture of distributed decision-making and personal interaction coexists with industrial engineering efficiency. Drivers learn the "340 methods," which include such details as how to hold the ignition key when approaching the vehicle and saving a second or two by fastening the seat belt with the left hand while turning the key with the right. At the same time, they have considerable leeway in deciding how to get their day's work done. Groups of drivers meet at lunch to make adjustments in their afternoon delivery loads and to discuss problems; supervisors who get customer requests for schedule changes will commonly ask drivers if the change will work and how best to accomplish it. Explaining his handling of a customer request to return later in the day to pick up a shipment, one driver typically says, "I'm not going to call my supervisor to ask if I should. I already know what he'll say."

This rosy picture is not a full-length portrait of the firm. Not every employee is a committed UPSer; understanding and cooperation are not universal. But trust, understanding, connection, and a sense of membership are widespread. They make the company work and give it a reputation as a good place to work. They are some of the indications and benefits of high social capital at UPS.

What Is Social Capital?

The World Bank defines social capital as "the norms and social relations embedded in social structures that enable people to coordinate action to achieve desired goals." Robert Putnam, the Harvard political scientist, describes it similarly. "'Social capital,'" Putnam writes, "refers to features of social organizations such as networks, norms, and social trust that facilitate coordination and cooperation for mutual benefit."[3] Our definition, which underlies our exploration of what social capital looks like, how it works in organizations, how investments are made in it, and what returns organizations and individuals can expect from those investments, is as follows:

> *Social capital consists of the stock of active connections among people: the trust, mutual understanding, and shared values and behaviors that bind the members of human networks and communities and make cooperative action possible.*

Social capital makes an organization, or any cooperative group, more than a collection of individuals intent on achieving their own private purposes. Social capital bridges the space between people. Its characteristic elements and indicators include high levels of trust, robust personal networks and vibrant communities, shared understandings, and a sense of equitable participation in a joint enterprise—all things that draw individuals together into a group. This kind of connection supports collaboration, commitment, ready access to knowledge and talent, and coherent organizational behavior. This description of social capital suggests appropriate organizational investments—namely, giving people space and time to connect, demonstrating trust, effectively communicating aims and beliefs, and offering the equitable opportunities and rewards that invite genuine participation, not mere presence. But even when social capital investments are made solely by individuals who develop ties with one another, many real advantages accrue to the organization as a whole.

Origins of an Idea

The term *social capital* first appeared in print in 1916 in a discussion of school community centers, and was subsequently taken up by academics and writers including Jane Jacobs (whose *The Decline and Rise of American Cities* describes values inherent in networks found in close-knit neighborhoods), George Homans, and John R. Seeley.[4]

In the past several decades, sociologists have given the concept additional academic credentials. Glenn Loury used the phrase in 1977 to describe the sources of certain kinds of income disparities, and Pierre Bourdieu, the influential French sociologist, described social capital as one of several forms of capital that help account for individual achievement.[5] In his article "Social Capital in the Creation of Human Capital" and in *Foundations of Social Theory*, his magnum

opus, Chicago sociologist James Coleman argues against the indi-
vidualist bias of human capital theory; that is, against the notion
that investments in people alone, regardless of the positions they
occupy or the networks they belong to, will generate significant
returns.[6] Sociologists' increasing attention to the development of
networks and communities, the transmission of norms and values,
and the meaning of collectivity makes an important contribution
to our understanding of social capital in cultures and organizations.[7]
As yet, however, most academics have had little to say about what
managers can do to increase an organization's stock of social capital. Their explorations remain largely theoretical or analytical. With
this book, we hope to contribute to a progression from description
to action.

In the realm of politics, Robert Putnam's landmark 1993 book,
Making Democracy Work, convincingly demonstrated the political, institutional, and economic value of social capital. Putnam studied cities
in northern and southern Italy to determine the source of differences
between the flourishing economy and civic culture of the North
and the relative poverty and economic backwardness of the South.
He concluded that the centuries-old social institutions of the North
that contributed to trust and connection between people and a
shared regard for the welfare of the community as a whole made the
success of the region possible. A lack of similar institutions pre-
vented the South from carrying out the cooperative efforts on which
regional economic success depends. In 2000 Putnam brought out
Bowling Alone, a scholarly yet provocative and stimulating account of
the causes and consequences of America's declining social capital.

The findings of comparative economic studies conducted by
political scientists at the World Bank and other global institutions
corroborate Putnam's thinking.[8] Why do some regions lag behind
while others thrive? Clearly some countries are more richly
endowed with natural resources than others, but institutional traditions, levels of trust and reciprocity, the rule of law, and the sense
of community are at least as important to a nation's health as the
available raw materials. The former Soviet Union provides an example of a state unable to take full advantage of its immense resources
(including the intelligence and talent of its people) because they lack
many of the required social institutions. At the turn of the twentieth century, Argentina was the seventh largest and most powerful

economy in the world. Now, 100 years later, it ranks sixty-fourth. Although that country is still blessed with natural resources and educated, entrepreneurial people, a century of untrustworthy institutions, political instability, and continuous attacks on community structures have taken their toll on economic health and social capital. As one of the World Bank's leading social capital champions, Michael Woolcock, states,

> Social capital provides . . . a fruitful conceptual and policy device by which to get beyond exhausted modernization and world-system theories and make potentially important contributions to questions of economic development. . . . Social capital's greatest merit is that it provides a . . . comprehensive multi and interdisciplinary approach to some of the most pressing issues of our time.[9]

Until recently, the term *social capital* has been applied almost exclusively to individuals and to social groups such as communities, neighborhoods, cities, regions, and nations. But enough commonality exists between these entities and businesses to suggest that social capital analyses of the former can teach us valuable truths about the latter. The idea of looking at social capital in firms and other formal organizations is relatively new—in part, perhaps, because mechanistic ideas of how organizations work have masked their deeply social nature. Henry Ford lamented, "Why is it that when I buy a pair of hands, I always get a human being as well?" But today, the variability or "humanness" of human beings, which disturbed the perfect regularity of Ford's assembly lines, is seen as a prime source of organizational value. As Geoff Mulgan notes,

> Many machine-like jobs are better performed by machines, and growing numbers of jobs require people to take initiative, to be creative and inventive. Even most daily interaction with machines is in truth interaction with other people. A more intensively social model of labour is coming into sight, where learning and work are no longer clearly separated and docile obedience is not enough.[10]

To Mulgan's *initiative, creativity,* and *interaction,* we would add *commitment* and *collaboration.* As Mulgan suggests, we are beginning to understand the inherently social nature of work. Human work is social to a much greater degree than people realize even today. Not only Henry Ford's cog-in-the-machine view of workers but the newer idea of the independent knowledge worker—including the telecommuter and the "road warrior"—turning information into useful knowledge with the click of a mouse, ignores or grossly underestimates the profoundly social nature of work. That contemporary idea either puts excessive faith in individualism or sees knowledge work as just another mechanical process—a kind of one-person assembly line where information goes in at one end and knowledge comes out the other. We are beginning to discover the centrality of social interaction—of trust, personal networks, and communities—to work of virtually all kinds. Etienne Wenger's detailed description of insurance claims processors in *Communities of Practice* shows the importance of social interaction to even seemingly individual information-processing tasks.[11] An anecdote about Franklin Roosevelt's personal physician suggests that the doctor's exclusive attention to one patient (something that intuitively seems desirable) may in fact have proved detrimental in some ways. Because the doctor worked alone, cut off from the experiences of seeing other patients and working with colleagues, he may have failed to learn things that might have extended the president's life. This despite his unquestionable ability and a conscientious effort to keep up with the medical literature. The examples could be multiplied. We are beginning to discover the collective nature of almost all work. To put it another way, we are beginning to discover the central value and importance of social capital to the work of organizations.

A social capital approach to organizational work differs from what we might call the individualistic or atomic theory of organizations, which recognizes a legitimate relationship of sorts between an individual employee and the firm—contracts, paychecks, and performance reviews document its existence—but ignores the networks of relationships among people in the organization and the less tangible elements of the employee-firm relationship: the human need for membership and identification, the satisfaction gained from recognition by peers, the pleasure of giving as well as getting help. It differs, too, from the currently popular idea of a work world defined by free agency—of independent "companies of one" drawn together for particular projects, collaborating over the Internet and going their separate ways when the project is done. Free agency hype and the social capital implications of that model of work are among the issues that convinced us to write this book.

Having worked with consulting organizations for years, we have become deeply suspicious of the "people, processes, technology" mantra ceaselessly intoned as a summary of the sources of organizational effectiveness.[12] While this triad improves on even more limited ideas (for instance, that businesses are solely about processes or that advanced technology alone can solve most organizational problems), we firmly believe that all of these notions leave out the essential connections among people without which purposeful cooperative work cannot happen. Some organizations have talented people, sensible and efficient processes, and the best technology money can buy and still perform poorly, hobbled by suspicion, rivalry, the chaos of rapid turnover, and the incoherence that results from people working at cross purposes.[13] In his *Knowledge in Action*, organizational psychologist Chris Argyris describes being called in to a Boston-based consulting firm stymied by lack of cooperation. Although staffed by the best and brightest from the top business schools, the firm neglected all the issues that we describe as having to do with social capital and was frustrated by its inability to realize the benefits of its collective talent. In another example, British Telecom's internal examination of the failure of its merger with MCI points to human dynamics and interactions, not flawed strategic or business models or the lack of individual talent, as the source of that failure. The authors of the BT report cite authors Marks and Mirvis on the 60 to 80 percent failure rate of alliances, mergers, and acquisitions to show that the problems experienced by British Telecom and MCI are common.[14] Success at bringing together two organizations with two (or more) cultures depends at least as much on social capital issues like trust, understanding, and equity as on strategic or technical issues, yet firm after firm makes the mistake of acting as if disparate groups of people can be welded together like machine parts. The BT report authors wisely recommend that the organization invest in a "robust cultural audit" as part of future merger decisions and preparations.

Social Capital Investments and Returns

Like other analysts using the term, we talk about social *capital* to emphasize that investment in interpersonal connections produces returns just as other, more tangible forms of capital do. We know

that "capitalization" can go too far. We are all familiar with financial capital and physical capital. Gary Becker and Theodore Shultz
have earned Nobel Prizes for their work on human capital, and we
may soon see a Nobel given for work on intellectual capital. Commentators also talk about "structural capital" and "customer capital." Not everything of value should be called "capital," but we firmly
believe that social capital is as real and important as other forms of
capital deserving the name. Like them, social capital can be demonstrated, analyzed, invested in, worked with, and made to yield benefits. Like them, it grows with effective use. As Harvard Kennedy
School Professor Jane Fountain remarks, "Social capital, like other
forms of capital, accumulates when used productively. . . . [L]ink-
ing cooperation to the economic concept 'capital' signals the investment or growth potential of a group's ability to work jointly."[15]
Robert Putnam explains how and why social capital accumulates:

> Stocks of social capital, such as trust, norms, and networks, tend to be self-
> reinforcing and cumulative. Successful collaboration in one endeavor builds
> connections and trust—social assets that facilitate future collaboration in
> other, unrelated tasks. As with conventional capital, those who have social
> capital tend to accumulate more—them as has, gets.[16]

This cumulative process underlies the value and power of social
capital and makes it somewhat difficult to discuss systematically.
Many of the elements of social capital are both cause and effect,
simultaneously its underlying conditions, indicators of its presence,
and its chief benefits. Take trust as a key example. Without some
foundation of trust, social capital cannot develop—the essential connections will not form. So trust is a precondition of healthy social
capital. Not surprisingly, high levels of trust also tend to indicate high
social capital. And the trust-based connections that characterize social
capital lead to the development of increased trust as people work
with one another over time, so trust is also a product or benefit of
social capital, and a source of other benefits. Deeply embedded in
the social capital life cycle, trust cannot be pinned down to one particular function. We believe that this book's lack of rigorous distinctions among social capital causes, indicators, and effects reflects the
organic and self-reinforcing nature of social capital and not (in this
instance, at least) the sloppy thinking of the authors.

Social capital exists in every organization, but in widely varying amounts. It can be depleted or enhanced, squandered or invested in. That social capital generates economic returns is one of the underlying messages of this book. In one sense, that point is obvious: without social capital, organizations simply cannot function. Our more useful point is that social capital can benefit organizations in particular ways. We explore those benefits throughout this book, and summarize them here as follows:

- Better knowledge sharing, due to established trust relationships, common frames of reference, and shared goals

- Lower transaction costs, due to a high level of trust and a cooperative spirit (both within the organization and between the organization and its customers and partners)

- Low turnover rates, reducing severance costs and hiring and training expenses, avoiding discontinuities associated with frequent personnel changes, and maintaining valuable organizational knowledge

- Greater coherence of action due to organizational stability and shared understanding

The returns on social capital for individuals and organizations are intangible as well as tangible, and those intangible returns are at least as important as the tangible ones. The familiar story of the online Eureka system used by Xerox copier repair technicians to share tips on solving difficult problems provides an example. Those technicians actually rejected an offer of financial rewards for contributing tips because the intrinsic reward of reputation and gratitude among peers was so much more important—a part of their personal identity, remarks John Seely Brown, chief scientist at Xerox. Getting paid for the tips would have threatened to trivialize that deeper satisfaction. Recent excitement about millions of dollars made by individuals in technology companies obscures an important truth: Work is not only about money, and those aspects that are unrelated to money can help organizations succeed economically.

Referring to the strong sense of self-worth the Xerox technicians get from recognition by their peers, Brown says, "If you can understand and tap that identity formation, then you are on the road to gold."[17] As his remark suggests, the various benefits of social capital complement one another: personal satisfaction and organizational and personal reputation are valuable in themselves, and bound up with competitive effectiveness.

Of course, organizations fail or succeed for many reasons; it would be foolish to present social capital as the only villain or hero of the story. Social capital is not *the* key to organizational success. Some firms succeed despite the negative effects of low social capital, although they often pay a huge price for it. Some firms with high social capital fail. Organizations are tremendously complicated and operate in complicated environments. And social capital is not a business strategy or a marketing plan or a substitute for either. It is not always even a good thing. Some firms have been damaged by high social capital that breeds unthinking loyalty and unquestioned shared beliefs—too strongly identifying with a group sometimes means mutually supporting ideas that are narrow or wrong. Too much warm and fuzzy gemütlichkeit can prevent people from challenging each other with tough questions or from engaging in the "creative abrasion" that Dorothy Leonard describes as a source of innovation.[18] Digital Equipment Corporation and Polaroid were both known for collegiality, a strong sense of employee membership, and humane management, but these aspects of their corporate cultures did not protect them from market misjudgments and strategic errors and may in fact have contributed to them.

In general, though, we believe that the effects of high social capital are overwhelmingly positive. Engagement, collaboration, loyalty, persistence, and even dedication are important benefits. The firms we look at here—UPS, Aventis, 3M, Hewlett-Packard, Russell Reynolds Associates, SAS Institute, Viant, and others—have made investments in social capital that enable them to attract and retain good people and help them do good work.

Hidden in Plain Sight

Social capital is so much a part of the fabric of people's working lives that it tends to be invisible, as the things we see every day and take for granted often go unnoticed. An old proverb notes that "the fish does not see the water it swims in"; similarly, we often fail to see the social capital that surrounds us. In broadest terms, we are writing about a subject that everyone understands and few discuss. The value of connections between people at work—the value, for instance, of getting reliable help from a colleague when you need it or knowing that your contributions to team success will be recognized and rewarded, the value of commitment as opposed to going through the motions—is self-evident in most people's daily lives. But organizations and those who study them often ignore these facts of life or reduce them to banal, apple-pie-and-motherhood mission statements. We know how important they are to our work, but organizations and business thinkers often behave as if they have no importance at all, as if, in fact, they don't exist and people leave their humanness at the door of the workplace. Arie de Geus of Royal Dutch/Shell remarks, "Whereas the management curriculum had no place for human beings, the workplace was full of them."[19]

Things happen as they do (or fail to happen at all) largely because of the ways those human beings in the workplace relate to one another. We have been to many management conferences where representatives of corporations described successful new initiatives. They laid out the conceptual frameworks, the organizational structures, and the technologies that allowed a team or groups to share knowledge, reduce errors, accelerate processes, and save the organization tens or hundreds of millions of dollars. The presenters seem generally honest and their figures more or less accurate, but they seldom tell the whole story. The hidden networks of connection, influence, and commitment that deeply influence the project are rarely mentioned, or are mentioned only in a reductive, dismissive phrase: "Of course, culture is important too." The daily experience of the people involved in the project remains invisible—who is helping or hindering the work, whether the changes that save time and money create a sense of accomplishment among participants or foster exhaustion and resentment, whether the project is perceived as an oddball anomaly or a model for change. In other words, all of the tension and texture of real work are left out.

Yet those social factors have a huge impact. During a break at a large conference, one of the authors asked a man who had presented his firm's flagship knowledge-management initiative at a similar meeting six months earlier how that effort was going. The presentation had shown it to be an unusually well-thought-out project that had quickly proven its economic value.

"It was canceled," the ex-project leader said.

"Why? I thought it was successful."

"It was," the man responded, "and the CEO supported it, but we never got the CFO involved. He resented being out of the loop and he wasn't keen on the idea in the first place, so he found a way to cut our funding."

This fairly familiar story suggests the obvious power of the social realities of organizations—realities that everyone who has spent more than a week in an organization recognize but that are usually omitted from management discussions, conferences, and the curricula of business schools that focus on structure, process, pure rationality, or some abstract, unitary concept of "the worker."

Not only social capital but the elements that define and support it are often invisible or ignored. The official organization seldom understands, analyzes, or even discusses the networks and communities integral to social capital, though recent work on knowledge management and communities of practice is finally bringing them the attention they deserve. Many organizations run into problems because they fail to heed the implied expectations and commitments of the unwritten social contract that defines the connection between an organization and its members. Although the terms of this "contract" are largely tacit, they are as important as explicit agreements about salary, benefits, and job responsibilities, and violating them can have powerful negative consequences.

Social capital may be hidden, but the damage caused by low social capital and the benefits to be derived from high social capital are visible and understandable. Our aim in this book is to make the invisible visible, to show how social capital is created and maintained in organizations and how it plays an essential role in making organizations work.

What Social Capital Is Not

Social capital is not about everyone in an organization liking and accepting one another; it is not about being "nice." IDEO, the highly successful industrial design firm, thrives on collaboration, mutual respect, and a shared understanding of how the work of the company gets done. It has high social capital, but that does not make it a gentle, uncritical culture. People who violate the organization's norms are typically frozen out of meaningful work, for example. Not invited to participate in the all-important brainstorming sessions, not offered help or even included in conversations, they often choose to leave the company.[20]

Nor is social capital about employees sharing details of their personal lives, erasing the line between work and home. Not long ago, the business section of the *Boston Globe* published a letter complaining that the writer's boss, having become convinced of the value of connection and community at work, had instituted a weekly meeting during which everyone in the office was required to tell the group one thing about their personal lives that no one else knew. This kind of coerced intimacy—the invasion of privacy that the letter complained about—is as likely to damage trust and connection as build them. Although friendships often develop at work, collaboration does not depend on coworkers being friends or knowing everything about one another.

Nor is social capital demonstrated or enhanced by lip service to equity and respect. Calling everyone in an organization an "associate" when in fact most have no decision-making power or direct participation in the organization's success merely breeds cynicism. Since social capital is about trust, relationship, and commitment, it thrives on authenticity. Hypocrisy kills it.

The Ties That Blind

As we have suggested, the effects of social capital are not invariably positive. The ties that bind can also be the ties that blind. The same social capital that draws members of groups together to perform useful work can also make groups clannish, isolated, narrow-minded, suspicious of outsiders, and even delusional. The close connections that help people work together effectively also characterize the old-boy networks that exclude talented women from important jobs, organizations that shut the door on members of particular ethnic or religious groups, and groups in which a strong sense of "us" includes and even depends on hatred for "them." In other words, merely having shared values and a shared worldview guarantees nothing about a group's quality, rationality, or usefulness. Loyalty and trust within a group may support cooperative efforts to achieve misguided or destructive aims, the members reinforcing one another's adherence to "norms" that the wider social context judges to be abnormal and even evil. Some street gangs, the Nazi brown-shirts of Hitler's time, and other close-knit hate groups all have extremely high social capital. Less drastic but still an example of how strong social ties can "normalize" aberrant behavior in a close-knit group are organizations—occasionally revealed by a whistle-blower—in which fraud has become accepted and acceptable, "the way things are done here." More commonly, members of a close-knit organiza-tion may support one another's misjudgments about the desirability of its products until the marketplace teaches them otherwise (a les-son sometimes learned too late, as the unhappy declines of Wang and Digital Equipment Corporation demonstrated).

These negative examples do not discredit social capital in gen-eral, any more than examples of clever crimes or destructive inven-tions discredit human intelligence. We sometimes use the phrase *high social capital* as shorthand for healthy, productive social capital, but we do try to stay alert to the issue of the ties that blind—the dark side of social capital. Our discussions of strong communities return to the issue of guarding against the dangers of clannishness, mutual delusion, and the normalization of deviance.

Social Capital and the World Today

If social capital has always been with us, and no organization can exist without it, why pay special attention to it now? Organizations with high social capital have survived for a long time without being identified as such, while paying little or no explicit attention to what the concept means. There are powerful reasons for writing and read-ing a book about social capital now, however, just as there are pow-erful reasons to analyze knowledge (which has also always been with us) in the context of business: because changes in organizations and the economic, social, and technological worlds they inhabit make an understanding of such concepts more important than ever. Just as knowledge, though always valuable, has become an increasingly critical element of organizational capability and worth, so too has social capital. What in the past could be taken for granted and sometimes even minimized can no longer be ignored or left to chance. This is true in part because organizations in a changing, highly competitive global economy need to make the most of their assets, of which social capital is key. More specific reasons have to do with the changing nature of work and the world.

THE AGE OF INTERDEPENDENCE

We are long past the time when any one individual can know virtually everything worth knowing.[21] We are even past the time when a single individual can know everything important about any global organization, or everything he needs to know to do his own work well. So belonging to the networks that can coordinate and enhance our necessarily limited knowledge has become essential. In the sciences as well as the corporate world, the individual genius, although not extinct, is rarer than ever. Even the individuals whose accomplishments have been recognized by Nobel Prize awards were supported by a dense web of predecessors, institutions, colleagues, and assistants.[22] Tom Boyle of British Telecom calls this the age of interdependence; he speaks of the importance of people's NQ, or network quotient—their capacity to form connections with one another, which, Boyle argues, is now more important than IQ, the measure of individual intelligence.[23] In many endeavors, collaboration—often involving numerous people in multiple locations—has become unquestionably necessary. Sociologist Walter Powell of the University of Arizona describes trends in biotechnology, a field in which the complexity and rapid pace of research mean that advances can only be made by large collaborative networks of experts. He cites the example of a paper on the DNA sequence of yeast chromosomes that lists 133 authors from eighty-five institutions.[24] The size and intricacy of organizations, the proliferation of critical information, and the increasing complexity of tasks make connection and cooperation—social capital—increasingly important.

The Engaged Organization

Although broad generalizations always oversimplify complex realities, we find important truths in the contrast between the hierarchical, industrial manufacturing firms that dominated most of the twentieth century and today's service-based and knowledge-intensive organizations. When industry meant repeatedly carrying out standard, well-defined tasks and workers were seen metaphorically (and sometimes literally) as parts of a machine, progress could still be made when the social networks and relationships of individual employees were ignored or even discouraged. In fact, those firms still strongly depended on social capital and sometimes suffered from a lack of it. Without some level of trust, respect, and generalized reciprocity, coordinated work of any kind is hard to accomplish. Still, as the comment by Henry Ford mentioned earlier suggests, a certain rough logic lies behind treating people like cogs in a machine when you only expect and want them to do machine-like work.

But very little of the work of today's knowledge firm is repetitive or mechanical. It requires responsiveness, inventiveness, collaboration, and attention. Judgment, persuasiveness, shared decisions, the pooling of knowledge, and the creative sparks people strike off one another all depend on engagement with the work and with one another, on the commitment that makes one genuinely a *member* of an organization rather than simply an "employee" (that is, someone used by the organization). Although we ourselves sometimes fall into the trap of talking about "employers" and "employees"—the user and the used—those terms really belong to the industrial-age model and are inappropriate to the kinds of work and working relationships we consider here. Today's most economically productive work is largely voluntary, in the sense that doing it well calls for a willing engagement of the whole self in the task. "Going through the motions" is insufficient when the motions are not prescribed but change as you go along. In our view, the firm is neither a machine with each cog firmly in place performing its clearly defined task nor an unorganized (or self-organizing) flock of opportunistic entrepreneurs pursuing their individual destinies. It is—it should be—a social organism of people willingly engaged in a joint enterprise.

These ideas are not new but they have not yet transformed the thinking or actions of all business leaders. Knowledge age or not, the mechanistic model of labor that sees only clearly defined, explicit, and visible tasks as useful work still has a great deal of power over organizational thinking and behavior. Although the knowledge revolution has popularized the idea of the value of intangibles and the intangible but deep value of exchanges of ideas and thinking time, the belief that "real" work occurs only when people are visibly busy persists, whether that busyness means tightening bolts on an assembly line or pecking away at a computer keyboard. Social activities from chatting at the watercooler to lingering over lunch in the cafeteria are still widely considered work avoidance rather than (as we argue) occasions for exchanging knowledge, and opportunities to forge and strengthen the connections that make work possible. Even the more sophisticated knowledge-age model that identifies people, processes, and technology as the linked elements of work ignores and therefore threatens the human connections that collaborative endeavors depend on. It too can invite a mechanistic approach, though the mechanism is more subtle. We are writing about social capital now because it is so important to the kinds of work we do today and because thinking about *how* people work has not entirely caught up with the nature of work they are asked to do.

There are also some particular contemporary challenges to organizations and their social capital that prompt us to take up the subject now, especially because we believe that deliberate investment in social capital can help organizations meet these challenges and even turn them to advantage.

The Challenge of Volatility

Organizations today face considerable external and internal volatility. Companies must attract and retain workers whose talents are often in short supply and high demand and who may be unexpectedly wooed away by competitors in "the war for talent." New technologies, mergers and acquisitions, and a global marketplace full of developing opportunities and competition continually challenge firms. To remain effective and sometimes even to survive, they frequently must undertake major internal change to respond to (or anticipate) change in their environments. Partnerships, mergers, acquisitions, and changes in products or focus affect who works for the company and how they work and may even modify organizations' aims and values.

This kind of volatility can erode social capital, which thrives on stable connections and adherence to the explicit and tacit agreements that bind people to one another and to the organization. Perhaps the most obvious example of disruptive change is downsizing, which degrades networks and communities and reduces trust, even among the "survivors." Although less pervasive now than a few years ago, downsizing remains one of the first ways management reduces cost. Or take the challenge to United Parcel Service traditions and values, documented by Jeffrey Sonnenfeld and Meredith Lazo in their Harvard Business School case, created by the need to hire information technology (IT) professionals at management levels in the eighties, an exception to the company's long-standing promotion-from-within policy and an apparent threat to the promise of equitable opportunity.[25] To preserve its social capital (or limit damage to it), UPS faced the double task of assimilating the newcomers—making them "real UPSers"—and moderating the loss or betrayal felt by old-timers when the rules changed.

The fact that the company seems to have succeeded suggests a key point: Volatility may threaten social capital, but high social capital helps organizations successfully weather its ravages. As the experience of firms including UPS, Bristol-Myers Squibb, Xerox, and Russell Reynolds Associates shows, community membership and commitment to a shared aim are more reliable weapons in the war for talent—especially the war to retain talent—than signing bonuses and the shaky promise of stock-option riches. Similarly, when organizations that undertake necessary changes understand, respect, and take steps to preserve the value of their existing social capital, the changes are likely to go better, because they are accomplished with the support of the members of the organization. In fact, the challenges of hard times or complex change can foster a sense of solidarity in crisis. High social capital helps firms retain their skills and coherence, even when change occurs that would disrupt or dispirit organizations with smaller social capital reserves.

Some commentators celebrate volatility as *the* new way to work, and an unmixed blessing. Not surprisingly, we disagree. For instance, we admit to skepticism about free agency, the idea that each individual is, in effect, his own company, selling his talents to whatever organization needs them at the moment. Examples of successful free agency exist, though they are relatively rare except in the exalted ranks of sports and show business, but the belief that organizations can consist mainly of free agents who come together temporarily to get work done directly contradicts our understanding of how social capital develops and functions. Coherence, understanding, context, trust, and continuity would all disappear in a world of individuals buzzing around in an opportunistic search for the most rewarding project. Such radical volatility necessarily threatens social capital.

The Challenge of Virtuality

The phenomenon of virtuality both challenges social capital and presents an opportunity to make valuable use of a social capital perspective. By *virtuality*, we mean any work carried out over a distance of time and space, usually with the aid of electronic communication. Telecommuters, virtual teams, and laptop-toting road warriors are obvious manifestations. By extension, we also include the concept of the "virtual corporation"—the organization made up primarily of individuals and groups electronically tied together to accomplish a particular task and dispersed when the job is done.

Virtuality has complex social capital implications, to which chapter 7 of this book is devoted. To a significant extent, we see reliance on virtual ways of work as a threat to social capital and believe that techno-utopians wildly overestimate the power of information technology to genuinely connect people. To the extent that virtuality reduces or eliminates the experience of sharing a work space and turns organizations into scattered, electronically linked individuals with little or no experience of being together in work, it will reduce social capital. But the story is mixed. Experience shows that the technology of communication, properly used, can strengthen and expand networks and communities rooted in more traditional sources. It is part of today's social capital landscape, not merely a drain on social capital. Continuing improvements in technology and the gradual absorption of new technologies into the social fabric of life and work will give them roles and influence that we can barely guess at today.

What we do know is that the technology of virtuality, with its power both to separate people and draw them together, calls out for examination from a social capital point of view. The growth of the Internet and the phenomenon of the mobile worker increase the need to understand how and why people connect with one another, and to insist on the social nature of work whether people are in the same room or half a globe apart. Our new ability to contact anyone and at the same time be connected with no one raises important questions. We believe that social capital insights can both define the natural limits of virtual work and help guide thinking about how to design the communications technologies of the future. John Seely Brown and Paul Duguid have contributed to our understanding of this issue in their book *The Social Life of Information*.[26] We hope to make a contribution of our own in chapter 7, on the challenge of virtuality.

What Investment in Social Capital Looks Like

Like other companies with high social capital, United Parcel Service makes a wide range of investments in this area. The company prefers to hire people who fit the culture, who share its core values of hard work, cooperation, and commitment, over those who may be more experienced but lack these valued traits. The belief in commitment has been so strong that the company only recently relaxed a rule that forbid rehiring anyone who had left the company. Orientation programs, taught by UPS employees, not outside trainers, emphasize values and norms along with skills and procedures. The still strong promote-from-within policy, virtually universal stock ownership, and distributed decision-making contribute to a sense of participation and membership. An annual employee relations index both tracks employee opinions on issues including fairness of opportunity and trust and signals the firm's commitment to those values.

The firm keeps its traditions, aims, and values alive in "legacy books" that recount the experiences and thoughts of its early leaders and a policy book, originally published in the 1920s. UPS's annual meetings of top managers include a "Jim Casey Night," when the founder's ideas are recalled and discussed in the context of contemporary issues. And people at UPS frequently tell one another stories about the company's past and present. Although large and dispersed and dedicated to efficiency, UPS remains largely a face-to-face, "conversational" organization, held together by personal contact. Its electronic systems track pickups and deliveries and carry other company data, but people get together to make important decisions, build relationships, and communicate about issues and concerns. One senior manager says, "We are not a memo kind of company." The district safety officer at the Watertown, Massachusetts, center, though he normally works regular daytime hours, personally attends the monthly Worker Safety Committee held at 3:15 A.M. during the package-sorters shift. CEO Jim Kelly told one of the authors, "I don't even know the phone numbers of the people on our management committee because I never pick up the phone if they're in the office. We just walk into each other's offices when we need to talk."[27]

The fact that they are woven into the fabric of daily work gives most of these investments their power. We do not believe that weekend team adventures, company picnics, or similar activities do much to enhance social capital. They may foster a new relationship or strengthen an existing one, and probably help more than they hurt. By and large, though, one-shot "bonding" activities are ineffective because they are brief and a thing apart from daily work. Social capital is mainly created and strengthened (and sometimes damaged) in the context of real work. The conditions and durable connections that we experience day after day have vastly more influence on it than special events and team-building exercises. (These exercises, if they are inauthentic—detached from the work context—can even be counterproductive when they highlight a hypocritical distance between the togetherness activity and the firm's real character.) Communities of practice are a popular and important subject today, and a critical part of the social capital discussion. Students of this phenomenon emphasize that communities grow out of practice; they are groups drawn together by common activities, not people who decide to do things together because they are friends or have played softball together or are pushed together by a manager.[28]

Students of communities also stress that they cannot be managed into existence. Recent work on communities and various aspects of knowledge management promote a kind of managerial intervention that encourages natural development, that orients rather than orders, that provides nourishment rather than blueprints. Some describe the difference in terms of a distinction between management and leadership. Some use the analogy of gardening or husbandry, the stewardship of an ecology as opposed to the construction or maintenance of a machine.

Successful investment in social capital—which of course includes investment in communities—demands this kind of organic approach. Networks of social connection, trust, and commitment cannot be manufactured or engineered, only encouraged. Social capital thrives on authenticity and withers in the presence of phoniness or manipulation. As many failed experiments in social engineering have shown, even well-intentioned and intelligent plans for model towns and cities and countries founder on people's refusal to do exactly what is expected of them, no matter how healthy or sensible that expected behavior is. In fact, the enormous dangers of social engineering might be considered one of the major themes of the twentieth century. Even efforts driven by noble motives have sometimes had dire results—unintended consequences run amok.[29] "Rational" human engineering frequently seems to kill the life it tries to "improve."

We do not suggest that leaders should take a hands-off approach to social capital. What corporate leaders can do to encourage, develop, and enhance social capital is in fact the main subject of this book. But their interventions must be based on a careful understanding of the social realities of their organizations and (even more difficult) a willingness to let things develop, even if the direction they take is not precisely the one envisioned. In short, they need to exercise what we think of as "light-touch leadership." Social capital investment is not for control freaks.

So a key principle for action is "First do no harm." Take care not to damage the social capital you have now. This advice is not nearly as passive as it sounds. It means, first of all, understanding the hidden social capital in the organization: It is easy to crush something you cannot see simply in the course of innocently moving around. It also means valuing the social capital you recognize. Almost every managerial decision, from hiring, firing, and promotion to putting in new technology to establishing revenue goals, setting travel budgets, and designing office space affects social capital.

All of those activities are opportunities for social capital investment or occasions of social capital loss. In fact (to qualify our own axiom), to do no harm is sometimes impossible. Economic and organizational realities often require drawing on and partly depleting a firm's social capital. The corollary to the axiom is to understand how much harm you are doing and to do as little as possible (to recognize, for instance, the damage done by downsizing, not just the benefit of reduced cost) and then to work to repair the losses that do occur.

Making Social Capital Visible

In December 1995, fire destroyed the Malden Mills factory in Lawrence, Massachusetts. The facilities and equipment that produced the company's successful polar fleece cold-weather fabrics were gone. Suddenly, 3,000 workers had no work to do. A few days later, CEO Aaron Feuerstein announced that he would nevertheless continue to pay their full salaries while the company designed and built a new factory.

Feuerstein's decision captured the attention of the country. Articles appeared in newspapers and magazines explaining how easily he could have taken the insurance money and retired, or used the fire as an opportunity to move his operation to a less expensive and less problematic city. Feuerstein was even invited to the White House, where he was hailed as a heroic and humane business leader. In an era of downsizing, when plants were closed and moved out of the country in the name of competitive efficiency, his action struck business commentators and the general public as rare, noble, and old-fashioned—a throwback to the days when people mattered more than profit and loyalty was prized over leanness.

That the public and the business world would consider Feuerstein's action so extraordinary and apparently "unbusinesslike" suggests that many people do not yet understand the value of social capital in organizations. It takes nothing away from the humaneness of Feuerstein's behavior to say that his decision made good business sense. His genuine concern for the welfare of the men and women who worked for him does not change the fact that the money he spent was an investment in the future of his business. By continuing to pay employees' salaries, he held on to a workforce that had proven its reliability and skill—people he had been investing in for years. By being loyal to them, he ensured their even greater commitment to doing good work for the company when the new factory was built. It is no accident that the company has an employee retention rate of over 95 percent, and that Malden Mills' reputation for quality products is undiminished. Feuerstein made an investment in social capital.

Perhaps *In Good Company* can help make that kind of story less surprising. In the chapters that follow, we explore key aspects of social capital in organizations. Our discussions of trust, networks, communities, social space and time, and communication consider the kinds of benefits organizations can derive from these elements and supports. We suggest reasonable investments in social capital that leaders can make. And we grapple with the challenges of volatility and virtuality. Much of what we say will probably seem like plain common sense. As we have mentioned, everyone who has ever been part of an organization already knows a lot about social capital. But as long as it remains unexamined, it will be undervalued, misunderstood, and often hidden. We hope to bring organizational social capital into the light of day.

2

❖

TRUST

If you suspect a man, don't employ him,
and if you employ him, don't suspect him.
—CHINESE PROVERB

ALMOST 80 PERCENT of the diamonds that come into the United States pass through the hands of the diamond merchants on Forty-seventh Street between Fifth and Sixth Avenues in Manhattan. One of the authors worked there as an office boy one summer forty years ago. Even at that (very young) age, he was struck by how little paperwork accompanied the buying and selling of huge fortunes in diamonds. No written contracts or receipts guaranteed the transactions. Prices were agreed on verbally; a handshake alone sealed the deal. Decades later, the business continues in much the same way.

The merchants' willingness to trust one another makes their business efficient. They are not only unencumbered by paperwork, but free of the related burdens that slow and complicate exchanges governed by written contracts: the legal departments that draft and approve them, elaborate monitoring structures, and formal machinery for ensuring compliance and punishing dereliction or fraud. Writing on "extralegal contractual relations in the diamond industry,"

Lisa Bernstein notes that "[b]y a variety of reputational bonds, customary business practices and arbitration proceedings, the diamond industry has developed a set of roles and institutions that its participants find clearly superior to the legal system."[1] She quotes an old dealer who says, "Many transactions are still consummated on the basis of trust and truthfulness. This is done because the qualities are viewed as good for business, a way to make a profit."[2]

Almost all of the several hundred merchants working in the diamond district belong to close-knit orthodox Jewish communities; their personal and work lives are closely intertwined. Most have known one another literally all their lives. That long, close relationship helps account for the bonds of trust among them. They have observed one another in schools, shops, playgrounds, and the synagogue as well as at work, with many opportunities to develop informed judgments about character and competence over time. Their being part of the same stable communities makes the potential penalties for betraying trust especially severe. In addition to being permanently banned from the industry, a dishonest merchant would be ostracized by friends, neighbors, and family, cut off from his religious and social community. Trust persists in the diamond trade because it is good business, as the dealer quoted above points out. If that alone were the reason, though, many businesses would boast similar levels of trust. Trust on Forty-seventh Street has deep roots in community and long-established practice. It cannot be injected into organizations and industries simply because it makes good business sense.

The Key to Social Capital

Trust is the one essential lubricant to any and all social activities, allowing people to work and live together without generating a constant, wasteful flurry of conflict and negotiations. In the event of conflict, trust is essential, as failed attempts at negotiation between countries and ethnic or religious groups sometimes painfully demonstrate. Trust is basic to human society, as John L. Locke says in *The De-Voicing of Society*:

Trust is like the air we breathe—it's basic to all human activities, so basic that the distinguished Harvard legal scholar Charles Fried declared that "in the end we pursue it for its own sake." A feeling of trust enables individuals to do things on their own—accept a date, buy a car, hire a house painter—or act in concert with others, whether as members of a small ad hoc working group or a stable community.[3]

Social capital depends on trust. The relationships, communities, cooperation, and mutual commitment that characterize social capital could not exist without a reasonable level of trust. John Locke says that trust "enables individuals to do things on their own," but in fact all his examples are of individuals or groups connecting with others. A complete lack of trust could only mean isolated individualism (or perhaps absolute tyranny). It is impossible to imagine an organization functioning without some trust among members. We see trust as a necessary condition of social capital, and its natural starting point.

Trust builds trust. Like a breeder reactor that makes more fuel than it burns, social capital uses trust to produce conditions that generate trust. So trust is the essential fuel of a social capital engine that produces more trust (among other things). Trust may be the clearest example of how, as we quoted Robert Putnam saying in the last chapter, elements of social capital "tend to be self-reinforcing and cumulative." It is at once a precondition, an indication, a product, and a benefit of social capital, as well as a direct contributor to other benefits.

The diamond merchants' practice demonstrates some of the benefits of high trust. It cuts the cost of transactions, reducing (in their case, nearly eliminating) the slow, expensive machinery of defining, monitoring, and guaranteeing compliance—the detailed spelling out of expectations and penalties, the tortuous process of enforcement. Trust supports cooperation in organizations, whether between two members of a diamond-trading firm who work together to evaluate quality and price, or among dozens or hundreds of participants in a research project, a community of practice, or a department. Trust also offers intrinsic rewards. Being trusted is a source of self-esteem and satisfaction in its own right. Working or living in a trustful environment, free of the frustration, anger, wariness, and disillusionment associated with lack of trust, is its own reward and increases loyalty and commitment.

As we have suggested, trust cannot be manufactured or wished into existence, no matter how advantageous it is or how essential to social capital. In this chapter we discuss trust in organizations: what it looks like; how it grows or declines; how organizations benefit from high trust; and what they can do to nurture it.

Understanding Trust

As one scholar put it, "in the social sciences, the importance of trust is often acknowledged but seldom examined."[4] In the past decade, however, social scientists have begun to examine trust more closely. Once thought of as a mostly passive quality related to personal and civic morality, trust has emerged as a key (even a universal) explanation of everything from corporate efficiency to national and regional success.

As background to our discussion, we need to make clear that trust or trustworthiness is not a uniform, indivisible quality. Trust is largely situational: a particular person may be quite trustworthy in one set of circumstances but not in another, where particular pressures, temptations, fears, or confusion may make him unreli-able. We trust some people to carry out one kind of work but not another. We may trust one colleague to deliver a presentation but not borrow our car, another to choose a business strategy but not a restaurant. Since someone's ability to carry out a task depends on competence as well as good will and basic honesty, not everyone can be trusted to do everything (though we tend to trust people who admit that they find a task difficult over those who appear overconfident in their abilities). A very few people we may trust with our lives; a few we may not trust at all. We probably trust many to be reasonably competent and straightforward.

Researchers do not agree on how people experience trust. Some propose a purely rational or intellectual approach. They argue that trust arises from a series of observations, in effect a set of trust-measuring experiments. One person interacts with another over time and judges whether his actions match his words. If the other keeps his promises, he is trustworthy; if he fails to keep them, he is not. Given enough time, this rational, experiential approach can lead to finer distinctions: "He can be trusted most of the time, but not when it means standing up to the boss" or, "I can trust him to get his work done on time but not to keep other members of the team informed." This description of the mechanism of trust is akin to the "rational actor/agent" or "economic man" approach that, while under considerable strain, still powerfully influences social science. It has an element of truth in it—empirical observations do affect our judgment—but any open-minded, reflective observer knows that people do not always or even often work this way.

For one thing, the rationalist "testing" view of trust assumes that the attitude of the observer or tester has no effect on the subject. Not true. Trust is a function of a relationship, not an immutable "quality" that one person has and another can discover. People respond differently to different approaches: when trusted, most tend to live up to that trust; when viewed with suspicion they sometimes justify that more pessimistic view. (Organizational leaders should take special note of this phenomenon.)

Also, people begin to trust or distrust each other as soon as they meet, before any transactions provide decisive evidence either way. Sometimes these early intuitive judgments even survive later proof to the contrary. The con men who get people to put their money into fraudulent investment schemes sometimes bilk the same people again and again, their charm and plausibility more convincing than the lack of promised returns. The fact that people are not purely rational seriously undermines the rational model. So does our need to trust people provisionally, before we have an opportunity to put them to the test, if we want to get anything done. We cannot test every salesperson, teacher, bus driver, or doctor before we put ourselves in their hands.

Francis Fukuyama labels immediate, intuitive trust "spontaneous sociability," while Karl Weick and his colleagues call it "quick trust."[5] It occurs almost instantaneously. Theorists often attribute it to an innate faculty or instinct that flourishes in individuals raised in healthy and nurturing environments. These initial judgments depend on how people look and sound and how they deal not just with the business at hand but with hundreds of "extraneous" activities, from how they shake hands to their ability to engage in small talk to whether they look you in the eye to how they respond to different people. Even apparently superficial attributes of appearance play an important role in how people judge trustworthiness. One of the authors recently spent time in a large urban hospital and overheard many judgmental comments by waiting patients about the appearance of various physicians—their age, gender, race, national origin, clothing, hair length, accents, even their footwear. "Can you believe he was wearing sneakers in the operating room?" was one such remark that clearly expressed doubt about the professionalism and trustworthiness of the surgeon. When gently queried by the author, the patients clearly indicated that these factors are used as "trust filters" even though there may be little or no logical connection between appearance and competence, honesty or reliability.

The quality and reputation of someone's workplace also have a powerful effect. We are more likely to trust a computer salesman in a well-known retail store than someone selling computers off the back of a truck; we put ourselves in the hands of a doctor affiliated with a good hospital more readily than one who opens a small office on a side street. The lack of such signals makes trust judgments on the Web a problem. Virtually anyone can create a professional-looking site at low cost, so judging by appearance can mislead. For this reason, the reputation of known brands is likely to be an important source of Web trust.

These various signals may prove wrong in individual cases, but we use them along with more intuitive "gut feeling" impressions to make trust decisions about the people we encounter as we go about our daily lives. The need to read a wide range of signals in making trust judgments helps explain the persistence of extensive business travel in spite of all the new communication technology in our lives. People doing deals, making transactions, buying and selling, need to evaluate the trustworthiness of their cohorts quickly, and still need to meet face-to-face to do so.

People also assume that members of certain professions (ministers and teachers, say) are likely to be more trustworthy than members of others (used-car salesmen and personal-injury lawyers). One of our closest colleagues, who was asked to be part of a major presentation to a potential new and important client, was told, "They'll trust you—you look and sound like a professor." No one at the presentation premeeting explained why merely "looking" like an academic should make a difference, since our friend was introduced as a senior consultant, or questioned the assumption that professors were more trustworthy than anyone else. On a similar note, one of the authors crossed the border between the United States and Canada, where he was living and teaching at the time, with a few books he had bought in New York State in the trunk of his car. He was supposed to declare the books, though as a college teacher he would not have had to pay duty on them. Not wanting to bother with customs declarations, he said he had nothing to declare. When the customs officer found the books, he turned a shocked face toward the miscreant and said, "You're a professor and you lied?"

In a more diffuse, less-powerful version of the trust among the orthodox Jewish communities mentioned earlier, ethnic groups, alumni of universities, and members of national fraternal organizations tend to trust one another more than "outsiders." For example, many ethnic groups who have immigrated to the United States have created collective institutions for self-help within a short time of achieving a critical mass of population. These institutions extend credit to immigrants who have little or no assets or credit histories—their trust based on the ethnicity of the immigrant rather than any individual experiences or histories. Bill Bradley drew on his fellow Princetonians to help his presidential campaign, especially within New York's investment banking community (a vocation that Princeton graduates have traditionally chosen). Trust decisions based on school affiliation, ethnic identity, and similar categories will sometimes prove wrong, of course: not every member of an ethnic group or college class is trustworthy. But to some extent those subcultures enforce trustworthiness because—though to a much smaller degree than the more intimately connected diamond merchants—they are networks through which news of dishonesty spreads, affecting the standing of the individual involved. The more dispersed and anonymous the "community," though, the less likely we are to trust other members deeply without some corroborating evidence.

Trust often grows from personal contact over time. To some extent, this truth blends the "rational actor" view of trust building with the recognition that we base evaluations of trustworthiness on many signals, including physical, emotional, and unconscious ones. Over time, we generally evaluate the trustworthiness of people on a combination of how reliably they behave, what other people think of them, and (more intuitively) whether they seem well-intentioned. There is no question that spending time with people generates trust. Sociologist Robert Putnam gives an example of the direct relationship between trusting other people and having opportunities to be with them:

> Evidence from the 1991 World Values Survey demonstrates [that] across the 35 countries in this survey, social trust and civic engagement are strongly correlated; the greater the density of associational membership in a society, the more trusting its citizens.[6]

The recent history of Poland provides an example of the importance of associational membership to trust and therefore to social health. Piotr Sztompka, a Polish sociologist, has published an analysis of how trust was restored in Poland after the fall of communism in 1989.[7] Sztompka demonstrates how trust in the fairness and effectiveness of the government fell calamitously when the victorious Soviet Army imposed communist rule following World War II. People invested trust only in the private sectors of life—family, church, and local communities. Large public institutions were no longer trusted or trust generating.

With the advent of the Solidarity movement in 1980, things began to change. Bringing tens of millions of workers together, this mass movement inspired and developed trust among its members. Solidarity became a trusted alternative to the distrusted government. When the fall of the Soviet government in Russia in 1989 left Poland free to go its own way, the associations developed through Solidarity provided a foundation of public connection for the renewal of civic trust. Expectations for the country were so high that dissension was bound to occur, but those difficulties did not negate the revival of trust. Free elections, a resurgence of the church, trade unions, and local government have made it more widespread.

Not surprisingly, trust has continued to grow in concert with growing social capital in the country. As productivity and wealth have increased, more resources are available for group and individual success, which in turn inclines people to be more trusting and trustworthy. Countries are far more complex than organizations and operate under differing principles, but Poland's trust-creating practices and policies are inspiring, and can serve to guide trust creation in U.S. firms and organizations.

Organizational Trust

Much of the trust in organizations—though not all—is the same kind of trust that exists between individuals, linked pair by pair through "quick trust" and judgments based on reputation and experience. Both first impressions and assessments made through experience and observation work within organizations as they do outside them. But organizational trust is not merely the sum total of personal trust relationships within the organization. There are valid, valuable ways to think about organizational trust as such and try to influence it. Indeed, we have found discussions of high- and low-trust firms that consider levels of trust throughout the entire organization, and several accounts of trust as a national or even a regional phenomenon.

One measure of organizational trust, for instance, is "span of trust." Surveys and network analysis tools can measure how far trust extends within a defined structure, in terms of the number of people to which trust can be "rolled over." Variations in span of trust are sometimes referred to as "thin" and "thick" trust, thin trust meaning widespread organizational trust and thick trust defining the stronger, shorter trust bonds within local groups. To some extent, certainly, people roll over their trust on the basis of recommendations of people they know personally.[8] This cascading trust is one source of organizational trust, and in some ways a bridge between personal and institutional trust. The trust brokers who vouch for people and make introductions help spread trust throughout an organization (and equally importantly, help distinguish between those who are trustworthy and those who are not). When the IBM Institute of Knowledge Management moved from a bland suburban office to Lotus headquarters in the more vibrant environment of Cambridge, Massachusetts, it faced all the issues of coordination and cooperation that moving an entire group raises within an organization—especially a large one. In this case, two IKM directors happened to have an established professional and social relationship with a then Lotus executive, Chris Newell. He acted as a broker to introduce all the key players at Lotus and roll over the trust he had developed in the IKM leaders to others at Lotus (who trusted him). He could assure them that those leaders would behave decently after they moved in—would not, for instance, scheme to grab valuable space from others in the organization once they had established a "beachhead" in the building. He could also tell them that, in his experience, those leaders reciprocated, offering help to those who help them. The trust bridge he built reduced the friction that the move would otherwise have caused, both the passive friction of an absence of help and the possibility of active opposition to an unknown "invading" group. The move could not have been carried out effectively without him; rolled-over trust saved time, money, and energy, and paved the way for new productive relationships.

In most cases, certainly, trust diminishes as it cascades. If you need someone to do an important and difficult piece of work, you will probably trust a person warmly recommended by a highly trusted colleague who knows you and your requirements well. If that recommended candidate is too busy to take on the job but says she knows someone who would do it well, you will not be quite as confident about the endorsement (in part because her ability to do the work does not guarantee her judgment about others; in part because she does not yet know you well enough to understand your needs). If, being desperate for help, you offer the job to that third person and *he* turns it down but suggests someone he knows, the roll-over effect will probably have weakened almost to the point of nonexistence. At best, you may take a chance on that recommendation if you believe that people in the organization generally do a good job.

In some high-social-capital organizations, the diminishing power of "he knows someone who knows someone who knows someone . . ." gives way to generalized trust. It will not be as deep as "thick" trust between close associates but can still be strong enough to aid cooperation and lower transaction costs. In some fortunate firms, many people do believe that others in the firm—solely by virtue of being part of the firm—are likely to be honorable, helpful, and competent, at least until they prove otherwise. So, for instance, a long-time employee of Hewlett-Packard says that he assumes that the HPers he meets for the first time anywhere in the world will behave cooperatively and share his aims. Very occasionally that assumption has proven wrong, but usually experience confirms his belief that people in the company can be trusted. In lower-trust firms, people are guilty (not to be trusted) until proven innocent; in high-trust firms, they are innocent until they prove themselves guilty. The stronger the generalized trust, the better for the firm in most cases, but strong generalized trust is rare. One CEO recently told us that he trusts everyone in the organization, but actual measurements show that trust is rarely both strong and widespread.

REPUTATION

Reputation acts in the middle ground between thick trust and generalized trust. When we have learned to trust someone we know well over time, her reputation in the organization as a whole will not influence us much. We even tend to explain away its negative features. ("She is not overcritical, she just has high standards.") But reputation gives us more to rely on than the generalized trust that judges pretty much everyone in the organization as probably trustworthy. Stanford sociologist Mark Granovetter notes that "the widespread preference for transacting with individuals of known reputation implies that few are actually content to rely on either generalized morality or institutional arrangements to guard against trouble."[9] An individual's reputation plays a significant role in assessing trustworthiness, especially in the absence of personal experience.

Reputation plays an especially powerful role in close-knit business communities such as venture capitalism, consulting, moviemaking, Web design, and publishing. As Robert Putnam notes, "Dense social ties facilitate gossip and other valuable ways of cultivating reputation—an essential foundation for trust in a complex society."[10]

The vast number of people in larger industries makes reputation a less powerful force, but not a negligible one. The tendrils of the reputational grapevine reach to the far corners of even large, dispersed organizations and industries. People who need information to make trust judgments usually find some way of getting it. Many of us have been in organizations when a person is promoted and all of her new subordinates scurry about trying to learn what they can about the new boss. What is her reputation in the company or in the industry? Much of the available gossip, stories, and innuendo—and much of what they want to know—has to do with the person's personal characteristics and perhaps most importantly with her trustworthiness. How much this matters is clearly contingent on how much you need to vest trust in her to achieve your own goals. It also points out how valuable it is for people to invest time and effort in building their reputation for trustworthiness.

High and Low Organizational Trust

Trust is essential to organizations, but no magic bullet. As we have said, social capital is not *the* answer to every business issue or a guarantee of success. Some organizations with relatively low trust but uniquely attractive products do well despite the toll that lack of trust takes on productivity and on the people who work there. Not all high-trust organizations do well. Sometimes high trust contributes to the ties that blind. Deeply trusting a leader with faulty ideas and misguided aims leads to disaster. But we believe that the effects of trust are overwhelmingly positive. Trust is a precondition of genuinely cooperative work. It lowers transaction costs and other organizational friction, and provides a foundation for other social capital benefits.

THE COST OF LOW TRUST

When people say life in their firm is "very political," they often mean that trust is scarce. The phrase suggests manipulation, secrecy, the triumph of shrewd calculation over hard work and raw power over good ideas, a place where you have to "watch your back"—a place characterized by what we might call "generalized distrust." Because these conditions are so frustrating, disheartening, and even infuriating for the people who work under them, consultants to such firms often hear about them early on in an assignment.

One of the authors consulted with NYNEX Corporation, the Baby Bell that has since been bought out by Bell Atlantic. Among consultants, it had a reputation for being extremely political. The author interviewed thirty or so managers in the privacy of their offices. In almost every case, the person interviewed turned the conversation away from information distribution—the subject of the consulting engagement—and raised a political issue. Some recounted their grievances against senior management or other managers; some complained about their job responsibilities or unfairly low status; some expressed anger at not being included in planning for a project that would affect them. Often enough, all these complaints mingled in a broad expression of dissatisfaction, demoralization, and distrust. The time and emotion devoted to these grievances represented a serious drain on organizational energy, not to mention the implications for cooperation and creativity. Low trust at NYNEX contributed both to its reputation as not a very good place to work and its relatively poor reputation among customers and other players in the industry.

Or take this example of problems caused by lack of trust described by David Packard in *The HP Way*. Packard worked for General Electric in Schenectady, New York, in the 1930s, when, he says, "the company was making a big thing of plant security." According to Packard,

> GE was especially zealous about guarding its tool and parts bins to make sure employees didn't steal anything. Faced with this obvious display of distrust, many employees set out to prove it justified, walking off with tools or parts whenever they could. Eventually, GE tools and parts were scattered all around town, including the attic of the house in which a number of us were living.[11]

In addition to creating an adversarial atmosphere, showing lack of respect for employees, actually encouraging theft and wasting resources on futile efforts to guard equipment, GE fell into the fundamental error—as Packard says—of not realizing that employees wanted access to those tools and parts to do company work on their own time. Being engineers, they enjoyed solving problems and took pride in it. GE should have encouraged them to take equipment home (as HP later did, its open storeroom policy a direct result of Packard's experience at GE). Clearly the policy did not destroy General Electric—it is doing fine today—but just as clearly, it hampered creative work and damaged employee relations at the time. Hiring the best, brightest, and most enthusiastic, and then treating them like untrustworthy children, is not sensible policy.

REWARDS OF HIGH TRUST

The more an organization depends on the creativity and collaboration of its members, the more important trust will be. At 3M, trust in supervisors and colleagues is a critical basis for the collaboration and entrepreneurship that have characterized the firm. As Sumantra Ghoshal and Christopher Bartlett remark about the relationship between trust and innovation in that company, "On the organizational trapeze, individuals will take the entrepreneurial leap only if they believe that there will be a strong and supportive pair of hands at the other end to catch them."[12]

The importance of trust within Russell Reynolds Associates and between the company and its clients can hardly be overstated. Clients entrust the firm with searches for CEOs, CFOs, and other executives likely to have a direct impact on their success. They base their confidence on the firm's reputation, on past experience, and perhaps on an ongoing personal relationship with a particular recruiter. Openness helps maintain that trust. For instance, senior recruiters who originate assignments do not imply that they will do most of the work themselves when they know another recruiter will. Longtime recruiter Alice Early describes how she has communicated this message to clients: "I used to tell my clients 'You don't want me to lead this assignment because I'm traveling too much. I just don't have time to do it right. What I *will* do is communicate with the associate leading the search every single day. I know the associate I'm asking to conduct the assignment will do a good job.'"[13]

The fact that she (and other senior recruiters) are able to give that assurance reflects the level of trust within the organization. Early comments: "If you don't trust that person with your client, she or he shouldn't be in the firm." This trust has many sources: frequent face-to-face office meetings, meetings of practice members, and even social gatherings that give people opportunities to know each other well enough to trust them. The habit of collaboration—built on initial trust—creates more trust as people work together over time. The principle of collaboration is supported by the words and deeds of leaders and the sharing of credit for successful searches. Unlike some law firms, where senior partners reap most of the rewards of work mostly carried out by young lawyers, recruiters who do the bulk of the work get the bulk of the credit.

Clarity and consistency about criteria for promotion also build trust—not only trust in the "system" but in colleagues whose advancement was due to performance, not patronage. According to Milan-based senior recruiter Riccardo Kustermann:

> Promotion requirements are out in the open. New recruiters are told what to expect and what is expected of them. . . . All recruiters know we have a 'grow or go' system. If they don't show continuous progression towards building a strong reputation in their particular area of focus, they will eventually leave the firm. When someone does leave, it comes as no surprise because during all that recruiter's previous years with the firm, he or she has had many evaluations and multiple opportunities with his or her Practice Leader or Area/Country Manager to take advantage of specific feedback.[14]

Trust grows from and contributes to transparency at the firm. Thanks to meetings, phone calls, weekly reports on active searches, and a global database that contains detailed information about work in progress, very little is hidden at the firm. "There is a lot of autonomy in how you spend your day," says one recruiter, "but your colleagues know what you're doing and what you're up against." Russell Reynolds President and CEO Hobson Brown, Jr., who says, "Everything in this firm works because of social capital," believes that the firm's trust-based collaboration is instrumental to its success.[15] One recruiter reports telling a client, "Our competitors are good. They'll do good work for you, but if you hire me, you'll get all of Russell Reynolds Associates. We have an ethic of collaboration that makes the collective wisdom of the entire firm available through me." This is a familiar enough sales pitch. Many firms strive for this kind of cooperation, but it only actually happens when trust is high.

Trust and Higher Purpose

A powerful sense of higher organizational purpose can sometimes foster trust. A sense of duty, patriotism, or idealism can help generate trust as well as commitment. People tend to trust institutions that have a "calling" beyond pure profitability; they are more likely to trust colleagues who share their commitment to an important goal (and in many instances sacrifice opportunities for a higher salary). This is of course not universally true. Some organizations combine noble causes with brutal suspicion and infighting, so we know we are on slippery ground here. But we have seen this trust-building mechanism at work at meetings with members of several branches of the U.S. armed services. The palpable patriotism and commitment to group effectiveness were overpowering and produced a very different atmosphere from those business meetings where self-interest and subgroup politics are never far from sight.

Recently one of the authors attended a meeting at the research division at Bristol-Meyers Squibb in Princeton, New Jersey. Like many pharmaceutical firms, BMS takes pride in the social value of its products. A video shown at the meeting told the story of Lance Armstrong, the bicyclist whose testicular cancer was cured by a BMS oncology product, and how he then went on to win the 1999 Tour de France, the most demanding and prestigious bicycle race in the world. The audience's reaction to this story made this meeting different from others we have been to, where organization profitability and growth were the heart of the message. In those meetings the lobby and dinner discussions were tinged with cynicism and a sense of opportunism ("where's mine"); at this one, palpable pride in the firm and a sense of joint commitment to a common effort animated people and brought them together.

Similarly, Johnson & Johnson's long-established credo helps generate trust within the organization and between it and customers. In its U.S. version, the credo begins, "We believe our first responsibility is to the doctors, nurses and patients, to mothers and fathers and all others who use our products and services." It then goes on to describe employees as the second highest priority, followed by the community and then stockholders. J&J managers say that this expression of purpose and values helps unite the members of the organization's scattered companies and create at least a presumption of trustworthiness. Johnson & Johnson's consistent and rapid worldwide response to the Tylenol crisis of the eighties demonstrated its values in action. The company's quick decision to pull all Tylenol from the shelves when poison was discovered in a few bottles that had been tampered with reinforced already considerable customer confidence in the company's honesty and values.

The Fragility of Trust

Trust can be quite fragile and volatile. Even deep trust that develops slowly over time can be damaged or destroyed, sometimes by a single act. Think of the long marriages irreparably hurt by a short-term infidelity. The same fragility can characterize the trust individuals have in institutions and organizations. One of the authors, brought up and educated to have strong implicit trust in the government, was teargassed at an anti–Vietnam War rally in Washington, D.C., in the late sixties. Listening to the radio news while driving home to New York, he was deeply shocked to hear a government spokesman categorically deny that tear gas was used, a lie repeated the following day in the *New York Times*. Twenty years of trust was seriously damaged by one statement that he knew to be false. The pain of disillusionment in a once trusted entity can make it difficult to trust again.

One dishonest action, even a seemingly small one, can cause measurable harm to an organization's social capital. We are familiar with a man who had worked for the same manager in a prominent financial services firm for nine years and had always trusted his boss. In the past year, however, he felt that the manager had overtly lied to him in his last performance review. His trust in this manager was seriously diminished. He demanded that all substantive interactions with this manager in the future be monitored, documented, and witnessed. Of course this raises the cost of these subsequent interactions, clearly demonstrating the relationship between trust and transaction costs. More critically, the atmosphere of wariness and mistrust generated by this kind of situation spreads quickly and easily. Those who trusted the subordinate also began to mistrust the manager, so his reputation was damaged and probably his effectiveness along with it. These examples suggest that organizations should treasure the trust they have and work hard to avoid actions that undermine it.

At the same time, well-established trust within an organization can have real resilience and (thanks to the "breeder reactor" effect) can generate additional trust. When norms of trust and reciprocity reach a critical mass, they keep growing. Trust eventually becomes embedded in the social fabric and becomes "the way things are done around here." This norm creates strong peer pressure on individuals to act in a trusting way, to reciprocate sharing and cooperation without any formal programs or pronouncements requiring the behavior. Trust is "in the air" in organizations, ever present, stable, and rarely remarked upon except when betrayed. It is an organizational attribute worth its weight in whatever currency you may desire. Unfortunately, developing it in environments that do not already have it is extraordinarily difficult. Distrust can spread also, similarly reinforced by expectation, observation, and experience.

Good behavior spreads by example and adaptation. Workers lower down in any organizational hierarchy look for signals from their environment about what behaviors in others have been rewarded and admired. When the qualities of those at the top—those who have been most rewarded by the organization—include trustworthiness, there is a good chance that others will copy that behavior, in part for self-serving reasons. (Examples of successful distrust and dishonesty also encourage imitation.) Good behavior also spreads through a "folk" or popular understanding of game theory. That powerful and influential social science tool claims to explain individual choice-making within a context of uncertainty. Robert Axelrod, a prominent game theorist, has shown how over time the most successful two-person game strategy is "Tit for Tat."[16] This involves copying your opponent's activities, whether "good" or not, so that a mutually beneficial equilibrium is achieved. Eventually, each player acts in a way he wants his opponent to act. The strategy effectively turns opponents into partners. While employees rarely delve into game theory mathematics, the folk understanding of Tit for Tat is well established and often serves as a way in which trust and cooperative behavior get reproduced. "Imitate what others do" and "Do unto others as you would have them do unto you" turn out to be closely related.

An established belief in the trustworthiness or dishonesty of a group or institution can be difficult to dislodge. Some people trust (and others distrust) the U.S. government in general. When they meet an individual employee of the government whose behavior contradicts their expectations, they consider her an exception. It can take many exceptions to dislodge a general belief. As Karl Weick points out, people "tend to be more interested in confirming rather than rebutting or contradicting" their expectations.[17] We consider and often only see the things that confirm what we already believe; we select and remember from the billions of events in the world the ones that support our opinions. This fact of human nature can work either way when it comes to trust in organizations. In low-trust organizations, examples of trustworthy behavior are likely to be ignored or interpreted as manipulation. In high-trust organizations, some lapses may be overlooked and examples of trustworthiness will be remembered and valued. This human tendency is a powerful argument in favor of maintaining an environment of generalized trust.

Investments in Organizational Trust

Acting to build and maintain trust is the most important social capital investment leaders can make. As we have emphasized, no one can impose or mandate trust, and developing trust in an organization that lacks it is difficult. But trust can be earned and encouraged, and leaders can take reasonable steps to build on existing trust. How do leaders foster trust? Through several kinds of authentic action.

BY BEING TRUSTWORTHY

Leaders set the tone of an organization; they more than anyone else establish and maintain its values and norms through their own actions. David Perkins and Daniel Wilson, researchers at Harvard University's Project Zero, remark, "Leaders are inevitably cultural architects whether they mean to be or not."[18] Trustworthiness can only be demonstrated, not asserted. The statement "You can trust me" sets off alarm bells for most people, and rightly so. When leaders behave consistently, fairly, reasonably, and reliably, those qualities spread through the organization. (When they are capricious, biased, or dishonest the organization reflects those traits instead.) What they do sets the tone of the organization. And, as we have indicated, they provide a lesson in what it takes to become successful in the organization.

Promotions to leadership positions act as firmwide signals; the fact that employee A won out over employee B shows people what values, approaches, and ways of working management looks for.

When promoted individuals have demonstrated their untrustworthiness, everyone absorbs a noxious lesson: crime does pay, or nice guys finish last. Such promotions contribute to a general atmosphere where trust is devalued and may even be considered risky and where unreliability or deviousness are seen as acceptable or smart. When trustworthy individuals are promoted, the organization proves that it values trust and that trust succeeds.

By Being Open and Encouraging Openness

Knowing who people are and what they are doing builds social connections and trust, just as secrecy tends to create suspicion. Openness and trust are tightly coupled. Without initial trust, openness is hard to come by—we need to believe that other people will not misrepresent what they know about us or turn that knowledge against us before we can be comfortably candid (for instance, about problems and failures as well as triumphs). Without openness, trust is hard to maintain. The radical openness regarding work in progress at Russell Reynolds Associates is built on and fosters trust.

Transparent and open promotion and compensation policies help build trust (and reduce suspicion). Our description of promotion policies at Russell Reynolds Associates provides one example. More transparent human resources policies go a long way toward eliminating those vague and murky promotion values that once dominated organizations. Terms like "executive presence" were often used not only to select friends and personal favorites but to exclude certain ethnic or racial groups. This self-reproduction of specific closed groups, which was quite prevalent in consulting and law partnerships, is a good example of the negative aspect of social capital. Again, such practices are not fertile ground for growing trust. In many firms, too, salaries are now "banded" in publicly available ranges to eliminate some of the traditional secrecy surrounding that most taboo of subjects—money.

Bob Buckman, founder of Buckman Labs, has made openness one of the foundations of his firm's operations because he believes that the trust it engenders and the cooperation that results are essential to the company performance he seeks. He has established three major principles of openness at Buckman Labs:

- Allow each individual to enter knowledge into the system.

- Give everyone access to the knowledge base of the company.

- Let every individual talk directly with those that have the best knowledge in the organization.

Even the acts of articulating and widely disseminating these principles help produce trust. They tell employees that the company has nothing to hide and that merit matters more than position.

The authors saw a vivid physical manifestation of transparency at the Grand Rapids headquarters of Steelcase, a major office products firm. Not surprisingly, these offices are a particularly innovative, open, and attractive environment. Pictures of every employee from the CEO to the secretaries are displayed on the walls along with attached biographies and personal statements concerning hobbies, aspirations, philosophies, beliefs, and wishes, as well as information about their current company projects. Whiteboards outside individual work spaces tell people about the work the occupant is involved in. As at Russell Reynolds, everyone knows what everyone else is doing. Even more surprisingly, many of the firm's records and files (within the bounds of legality and propriety) are literally in open files in the small open offices of the CFO, CEO, and COO. When we asked about dangers inherent in this approach, we were told that the practice demonstrated the trust the firm had in its employees and that there had not been any significant abuse of the system.

Letting employees share their knowledge with peers in other firms, even when their individual firms compete with one another, also builds and demonstrates trust. We were first struck by how far this approach has gone when were developing our first multiclient programs eight years ago. While a few firms chose not to participate in our program if competing firms did, more joined *because* others from their industries attended. We had been used to seeing scientists and technologists from competing firms mix and mingle at established scientific conferences and academic conclaves. We had seen marketing and finance educational events draw participants from competing firms. Now we were running a program on working with corporate knowledge. Was there ever a subject less likely to be shared? Yet the participants did share. (Many still do in a similarly structured program at the IBM Institute for Knowledge Management). Within the bounds of business judgment (boundaries that seem to get wider and wider) we see many organizations trusting each other enough to learn from one another in often surprising ways.

Openness helps trust and cooperation spread both within firms and through an entire industry or region. Indeed, an influential book by AnnaLee Saxenian argues that the ascendancy of Silicon Valley over Massachusetts's high-tech development belt along Route 128 was due in part to the continuous meeting, sharing, and talking done in the many restaurants and watering holes in open, high-trust Silicon Valley versus the relatively closemouthed culture of Route 128, which had to do partly with secrecy imposed on defense-related projects and partly with traditional Yankee reticence.[19] Of course, weather, traffic patterns, and other factors play a role too. Both authors live within a mile of Route 128; while we aren't particularly closemouthed, we agree with Saxenian's general assessment. The far greater interorganizational trust and openness manifested out West has clearly played a significant role in the region's success.

John Seely Brown and Paul Duguid discuss this growing trend in *The Social Life of Information*. They put it in the context of how organizational knowledge can be "leaky"—that is, pass readily from an organization to those outside—as well as "sticky"—in other words, fail to move to other groups in the organization. Much of the "leakiness" comes from the trust between individuals in different firms, and has three main sources. The first is a policy of openness based on the belief that the organization will gain more in new learning than it might lose in lost proprietary knowledge. The second is that the current trend toward "co-opitition" frequently makes it difficult to know who your real competitors are.[20] IBM, an obvious example, sells technology to many firms that its service business competes with in the open market. The third principle is that these activities are unstoppable, given the omnipresent Web and the culture it brings with it of increasingly informal business practices. Why buck the trend? The costs of control and monitoring costs far outweigh their elusive benefits. Perhaps, too, a lack of openness is the single most negative signal a firm can send to the bright young employees it hopes to attract and keep.

By Trusting

By and large, as we have suggested, people tend to be pretty much as trustworthy or devious as you expect them to be. Assume that they will try to get away with doing as little work as possible, and many will. Measure their work by the clock, and they will watch the clock and go home when they have put in their time. Assume, on the other hand, that they are capable, conscientious, and engaged, and most will prove you right. We know these things from experience, and many of us have been on both sides of this familiar dynamic. Here is an example from one of the authors while in his youth:

> One of the boys in my class at junior high school was a troublemaker—not dangerous or destructive, but everyone knew he was a clown who disrupted classes and took no interest in the work. At the beginning of the year, teachers warned him, "I've got my eye on you." Every teacher except one. On the first day of school, our English teacher read a poem and then asked him—the troublemaker, of all people!—for his opinion, asked seriously and even respectfully, more like one person to another than teacher to student. The rest of us were shocked. Didn't he know what a troublemaker this kid was, what a clown? In fact the troublemaker made some joke about the poem. We waited for the teacher to let him have it. Instead, he acted as if the joke were a reasonable response and thanked him. The next time the teacher asked him about a poem, the troublemaker gave a more thoughtful answer than any of us imagined he was capable of. He became one of the best and best behaved students in the class (though he lived up to his reputation as a troublemaker in his other classes).

We feel that Abraham Maslow, a founder of humanistic psychology, was right. Most people derive a substantial part of their self-esteem from their work and work life. They rarely intentionally do work badly. Leaders help build social capital by trusting employees, by assuming that they care about doing their work well. The "HP Way" has been described as "policies and practices that flow from a belief in people's desire to do a good job," and many of the management policies that made Hewlett-Packard such an unusually attractive and successful working environment for so long are based on trusting the good will and commitment of employees. The principle shaped the company's flextime policy, which states that "flextime is the essence of respect for and trust in people. It says that we both appreciate that our people have busy personal lives and that we trust them to devise, with their supervisor and work group, a schedule that is personally convenient yet fair to others."[21]

Packard's GE example, mentioned earlier, illustrates the futility of not trusting and some of the damage it can cause. Extensive monitoring engenders distrust. Organizations that make extensive efforts to keep a watchful eye on employees that they fear are trying to get away with something are often surprised that their suspicion is reciprocated: their employees become watchful too and strictly hold management to negotiated rules. At one time, the U.S. auto industry provided an example of this kind of wasteful standoff of mutual distrust. One of the authors once took a job in a state agency after having taught at a university for several years. He was so taken aback by the strictly proscribed coffee and bathroom breaks that he thought at first people were joking about them. They weren't. The constant mutual monitoring for compliance by union and management was so wasteful and fatuous that he soon left the position.

Appropriate and respectful monitoring can sometimes support rather than destroy trust. Several studies have shown that careful policies can help enforce trust without also being massively bureaucratic or controlling. But the most common enforcement mechanisms for trust are social. Whether in a community, an organization, or an industry, few experiences are as painful as the social ostracism, shame, or disgrace that can attach to a person who has broken trust with his or her colleagues. And few are as satisfying as demonstration of mutual trust.

MATERIAL INCENTIVES

Given the deeply social nature of trust and its necessary authenticity, direct economic incentives are not as useful as other trust promoters. Nevertheless, the right kinds of material benefits can help promote trust. IBM provides an interesting example that one of the authors experienced firsthand, since the company reworked its bonus structure while he was a manager there. IBM went from bonuses based strictly on individual performance to bonuses significantly influenced by group and firm performance. Not surprisingly, this change has produced the intended results of a greater propensity to cooperate and a more palpable sense of group identity. While we believe that self-interest is less powerful than other motivating forces, it does have an effect: individuals are more likely to help the group if they benefit financially from better group performance. The new bonus system in fact actually changes the terms of self-interest, making it less competitive and individualistic. Trust grows because the new approach reduces the barrier erected by internal competition and a "looking out for number one" attitude, and also—importantly—because the experience of group work that the new system promotes increases trust by bringing people together more and allowing the social forces we have described more opportunity to come into play.

Building on the Foundation

The interdependence of work in today's knowledge economy and the fact that knowledge work requires people to engage their intelligence and imagination in the joint effort explain why Peter Drucker says, "Organizations are no longer built on force but on trust."[22] Force can only compel compliance, and compliance is not enough. Commitment is required, and commitment cannot exist without trust.

We believe that trust has always been important. In the days when industrial production was king and the factory model prevailed, it was probably easier to make sure that work got done in low-trust environments, but the cost of low trust in the auto industry and elsewhere was significant. We believe, with Drucker, that trust is more essential and more valuable today. Our whole argument for the value of social capital makes that point, and trust is the foundation of social capital, of connection and commitment.

The glue that holds networks and communities together includes several ingredients. Shared interests and shared tasks are among them. Trust is the key ingredient. Shared interests and tasks can help develop trust, but when trust is lacking or has been betrayed, no amount of enthusiasm for a subject or advantage in joint work can hold these collective entities together.

3

❖

NETWORKS AND
COMMUNITIES

You may have the greatest bunch of individual stars in the world,
but if they don't play together, the club won't be worth a dime.
—BABE RUTH

O NE OF THE AUTHORS was invited to attend a meeting
in New York last winter. The meeting organizer had worked
with him before, when they were brought together by a
mutual acquaintance. (That connection also derived from another,
earlier connection, of course.) The mutual acquaintance and the meeting organizer happened to work in offices in the same building in
Manhattan. Several people with, no doubt, similar stories to explain
why they were there, had flown over from London; about half the
attendees lived in New York, and one—the author—had come down
from Boston. The subject we had gathered to discuss was how organizations would soon be procuring materials, components, and talent through open Web-based systems, allowing individuals and
companies throughout the world to compete on an equal footing.
Drawn together by the power of existing relationships, we contem-
plated a system that denied their importance.

Mainstream economists and many "new economy" writers seem
to believe that firms and the individuals who run them exist in a
social vacuum, devoid of ties, histories, loyalties, or values that

might influence their actions. They see businesses and their leaders as continuously looking for the best deals on materials and people, ready to switch suppliers or partners the minute a marginally better option comes along. As in the case of that New York meeting, they describe the advantages of open procurement systems that publish requests for parts and services on the Web and allow organizations to give the work to whatever organization in the world responds with a bid that promises the best combination of price, quality, and speed.

During a recent speech, Mark Walsh, the CEO of VerticalNet, cautioned new-economy advocates against believing that organizations really work or can work through this kind of unbounded, moment-by-moment striving for efficiency.[1] VerticalNet provides e-business infrastructures to some gritty, down-to-earth industries. Walsh specifically noted how all the major players in the solid-waste-disposal industry have known and dealt with each other for many years. Their long experience of one another has built robust networks of relationships and a deep understanding of industry players' reputations for reliability, honesty, and quality. Walsh comments, "A technology vendor is crazy if he or she feels that these firms will overthrow these relationships simply by putting new technologies in place. The technologies may make existing relationships more efficient, but they will not transform them."

These warnings from an experienced dot-com executive suggest how social capital works in industry networks, clusters, and ecologies as well as within firms, and how powerfully important these connections are. Brian Uzzi, a sociologically oriented business professor at Northwestern University, has done influential studies on the importance of internal social structures and industry networks to firms in two fragmented industries (that is, industries composed of many small businesses rather than a few giants). These robust social connections give the garment industry in New York City and middle-market banking in Chicago advantages of access, reliability, understanding, and "special treatment" that they would not have otherwise. Uzzi says, "Organizations gain access to special opportunities when connected to their exchange partners through embedded ties."[2]

In sociology and economics, the word *embedded* conveys the idea that economic and social activities are not "pure" transactions but are strongly influenced by the past and present social and cultural environment of the actors. This perspective helps explain the importance of social capital. People do not always look for the optimal economic exchange, the best knowledge, or the greatest skill when they seek colleagues, partners, or suppliers. Their own past experience and the experience and norms of their organization or group powerfully shape their choices. The reliability and comfort of established ties—experience-based confidence that the connection will "work"—influence their decisions, along with the intrinsic pleasures of contact with acquaintances and friends—the pleasures of loyalty, reciprocity, and even affection.

The Role of Social Groups

Human beings are social animals. We come together two by two in friendships and marriages; we form families and teams and the larger aggregations of practices, communities, societies, and nations. These groups assemble to achieve distinctive aims and to provide the satisfactions of sociability. Sociology, psychology, and political science have long studied social groups and generally recognize their centrality to what people do and how they feel about themselves and the world. Management thinkers, influenced by economists, have been slower to see the importance of social groups in organizations. They have looked at official organizational units over less formal structures, or have focused on individual workers rather than the groups they belong to.

Networks and communities are at once the source and shape of social capital in organizations, the primary manifestation of cooperative connections between people. Analyzing them reveals information about existing social capital; supporting them encourages social capital growth. They are a prime source of a sense of membership and commitment, the places in organizations where people feel most at home and most responsible for one another. They are sites of organizational learning and the main places where knowledge develops. Almost all the theorists who write about social capital make networks (and their close relations, communities and practices) central to their analyses. Some even define social capital solely in terms of networks. Hendrick Flap, for instance, calls social capital "an entity consisting of all future benefits from connections with other persons."[3] While we consider this too narrow a view to be entirely useful, it is not hard to see why networks play such a prominent role in social capital discussions. Social capital is about connection, we have said, and networks are how connections between people most clearly manifest themselves.

As long ago as the 1950s, a researcher found over ninety definitions of *community* in the social science literature alone; *network* can be defined in even more varied ways.[4] These many definitions create the danger of the words meaning whatever you want them to, although, interestingly, virtually all definitions of *community* are positive. Several decades ago, Raymond Williams stated that it was the only social theory term in circulation without any negative connotations whatsoever.[5] As alienation has increased in organizations, it is no surprise that the idea of workplace communities has become a popular subject. But the presumption that communities are invariably good is wrong. Sometimes a community harms the organization or society it exists in. Excessively insular communities can fall prey to shared hatred and mutually reinforcing delusions—the ties that blind.

In both popular and scholarly literature, networks are often conflated with communities and practices. They are not the same, but we plan to do some conflating ourselves after making a few distinctions.

Both networks and communities are groups of people brought together by common interests, experiences, goals, or tasks; both imply regular communication and bonds characterized by some degree of trust and altruism. Communities are generally more concentrated and focused than networks. Communities generally have a center of gravity that may be a physical location (as in the case of a village community) or a shared work domain (a community of practice). A network needs no such center. Communities enforce norms, something networks are probably too diffuse to do consistently. A community, according to Etienne Wenger, is a group of people "mutually engaged in actions whose meaning they negotiate with one another."[6] Though there may be some ambiguity about the membership of particular communities, they are typically *closed* in some sense: defined by a separation between those inside and outside the community: "us" and "them." The members of a community usually all know one another at least to some degree. A network is generally more *open*, an interlocking web of connections.

Individuals in the network know the people they have direct contact with, but they do not necessarily know their contacts' contacts.

Nevertheless, networks and communities often overlap to considerable degrees. The alternative use of the terms is not mere sloppiness but a recognition of how much they do have in common. A great deal of detailed work on the shape and nature of communities of practice has been done—by the Institute for Research on Learning, by Wenger, by Xerox PARC, and by the Institute for Knowledge Management, for instance. That depth of analysis is beyond the scope of our book. For the sake of our discussion, we use the terms somewhat interchangeably.

The Basics of Communities and Networks

Francis Fukuyama defines a network as "a group of individual agents that share informal norms or values beyond those necessary for ordinary market transactions."[7] This definition suggests, for example, that all individuals who donate over $1,000 to their firm's United Way drive are a network. Simply working for a given organization would require only the norms and values of participating in a labor market and its transactions. Even giving $50 or $100 might be interpreted as almost a necessity of employment or at least of being a good corporate citizen. Contributors of $1,000 or more will most likely have a more distinct set of common informal values and norms that would make them a separate "network," according to Fukuyama's definition.[8]

There is something missing here, though—the sense of active connection and affiliation that seems an essential part of a functioning network. If I contribute $1,000 to the United Way and so does John Smith in another department, we might have a lot in common and we might very well establish a relationship if we got to know one another, but the mere fact of our behaving in the same way does not, we believe, usefully make us part of the same network. A new sociological theme and a lesser but influential one in economics adds the elements of emotion and affiliation to standard network theory and makes it more recognizable, accessible, and useful.

Merely knowing a lot of people is not necessarily the same as being part of a network. Almost everyone "knows" as many as 2,000 people in some limited sense, and most of us have at least a nodding acquaintance with perhaps 2,000 more. But nodding to someone as you pass or even stopping to chat when you meet them on the street still does not make them part of your network. Network membership is a more active attribute. It requires some investment in time, energy, and emotion. It includes the strong potential for reciprocity.

In some sense, networks are not especially hard to understand. Almost everyone can easily answer correctly framed questions about their networks and tell who they know, how well they know them, and what they get out of knowing those people. We all build our individual networks by investing some significant proportion of our time, money, energy, and emotion in our connections with others. While the payback for this investment may not be as well defined as a municipal bond, it has the potential of being far more valuable in both tangible and intangible rewards.

Network Value

Networks form because people need one another to reach common material, psychic, and social goals. Mutual aid and generalized reciprocity are common to all functioning networks. But being part of a network must to some extent be an end in itself rather than solely the means to an end. Most of us have met people who so transparently and persistently use network connections for their own advancement that the network eventually rejects them. They "use people" or "only care about number one," their interest in others (except as stepping-stones) is feigned or nonexistent. In part, this is a problem of a lack of reciprocity, but it also has to do with the perhaps paradoxical fact that networks are more valuable and robust if you are in them not only for the value you get out of them. Supernetworkers like Lois Weisberg, commissioner of cultural affairs for the City of Chicago, are so well connected in part because they love connecting with people; they are social people for whom connection is its own reward.[9] Weisberg is a key player in many distinct networks, who connects and is connected to literally thousands of people who do not necessarily know one another.

We once asked a group of consultants what they would rescue first from their offices in the event of a fire—a fairly well-known method for discovering what people value. We stipulated that the offices of the executives we put this question to held items of monetary value, such as artwork or expensive furnishings. Almost without exception, however, the executives named whatever held their contact information—the Rolodexes, address books, and Palm Pilots they used to get in touch with the people in their networks.

A basic tenet of almost all social capital theories is that a network is one of the most powerful assets that any individual can possess. It provides access to power, information, knowledge, and to other networks—the totality of which provides a much better indicator of how "well-off" one is than many more acknowledged sources of wealth or advantage. Anyone with a college-bound teenager in the home understands the pressure to get one's child into the "best school." Often this means the most selective school, and this quite powerful push is not based solely on academic distinction. Many "lesser" schools have equally fine teachers and facilities, but "top" schools offer more and better opportunities to start building one's networks. One reason parents get so involved in the college search process is that this unromantic and self-interested view of campus life resonates with few teens.

The authors have a friend who went to Stanford University for his M.B.A after ten years as an academic. The amount of time his fellow students devoted to social activities surprised him. They played golf together and took part in the consulting club and were generally far more social than his fellow graduate students were when he was getting a Ph.D. in sociology. That greater sociability may well have reflected a basic character difference between most business and sociology students, but the Stanford students were also more aware of the value of investing in social networks as a foundation for later success. As our friend ruefully stated later on, "They knew what they were there for: building networks."

"It's not what you know, it's who you know" is often said cynically or bitterly. The adage expresses the unfairness of people succeeding thanks to personal connections rather than ability, knowledge, or hard work. The bitterness has some justification.

There is no question that old-boy networks and the like have helped people of little talent or dedication while locking out individuals who have the skill and desire to do good work. In *Getting a Job*, Mark Granovetter documents the overwhelming percentage of high-paying jobs attained through personal contacts, not want ads or cold contacts with human resources departments.[10] But the antidote to this kind of unfairness is to expand influence networks, not eliminate them. Elimination would be both impossible and unwise, given their legitimate functions and the fact that they are so integral to how people operate in the world. Organizations hire people through personal networks not simply because they want to take care of their friends but because—as we have said in earlier chapters—trust, reputation, and shared values are so important. Those qualities are hard to detect through resumes and interviews, so personal acquaintance and personal recommendation remain powerfully important. The way to increase fairness and bring organizations the talent they need is to create more networks and expand existing ones—not to deplore the fact that deals are made on the golf course, but to increase access to golf courses.

This kind of networking starts early, of course. How do high school and college-age kids from prosperous suburbs get decent summer jobs? In many cases, their parents call friends who are influential in organizations or know someone who is. Sometimes a well-connected college teacher introduces a student to an employer. Lois Weisberg recognized the importance of these kinds of networks and decided that the federal money being used for programs that put poor kids to work cleaning up city streets did little good.[11] "I don't believe poor kids can advance in any way by being lumped together with other poor kids," she said. She raised money to create an arts program that brought together low-income kids, middle-income kids, and professional artists—a program that created new social networks as well as student artworks, and has now been copied in cities around the world. "Poverty is isolation," concludes Malcolm Gladwell, in a profile of Weisberg he wrote for the *New Yorker*.[12]

The value of networks to individuals is only part of the story. Networks are key and critical components of any organization's stock of social capital. As we (and others) have said, social capital value accrues to organizations from people's efforts to develop their individual social capital. Though network building mainly happens between individuals, it contributes to an organization's social capital. Many of the benefits individuals derive from networks and communities—a sense of membership and purpose, recognition, learning, and knowledge—can also pay huge benefits to the organization.

MEMBERSHIP

Networks help people develop their identities. From grade school to retirement villages, the people we hang out with help us determine who we are. We live in our networks. Susan Stucky of the Institute for Research on Learning often says that anyone who went to high school knows a great deal about network theory, at least intuitively.[13] As we discuss elsewhere, people who identify with one another in networks develop common stories, frameworks, and responses. Ask several veteran consultants or investment bankers about their worst plane trip. The stories seem to merge into one common tale of woe. Verbal codes develop in durable networks within organizations like thick undergrowth, impenetrable to outsiders but home territory to members. Like legal, academic, or medical jargon, these vocabularies exclude outsiders, binding insiders together and making conversation more efficient.

Membership implies connection: the trust, understanding, and mutuality that support collaborative, cohesive action. It implies commitment to the group and the work, cooperation, and the willingness to do more for a job that is not "just a job." A sense of membership opens the door to the intrinsic rewards that John Seely Brown identifies as so important to personal satisfaction and organizational success.[14] People work to make money, but not only for that reason. The recognition and praise from colleagues and a sense of belonging to something are also very important and foster commitment and self-esteem that a good salary alone cannot guarantee. (Freud identified both work and love as essential to mental health.) Once again, Abraham Maslow is correct. Once a person achieves adequate financial success, he or she strives for other types of rewards in a hierarchy of needs.

People are loyal to their networks and communities. Those are the groups they identify with, draw sustenance from, and create their work identities around. When asked why they stayed with their current employers, several successful consultants we know emphasized their work community, the coworkers they spent time with, the individuals who were both colleagues and friends. In part because a sense of membership makes it less likely that valuable employees will be lured away by competitors offering higher salaries, this understanding supports longevity in organizations. Of course money counts, and some offers seem too good to refuse, but the greater the sense of membership and its intrinsic rewards, the higher the threshold of that irresistible offer. In an economic environment where competition for talent is fierce and retaining talent is important and difficult, fostering membership becomes especially important.

GROUND TRUTH

One source of the sense of membership is coming to know what the group knows—sharing the skills, practices, knowledge, language, and stories of the group. Networks and communities teach newcomers what we can call the "ground truth" of the organization. *Ground truth*, a phrase coined by the U.S. Army, refers to the complex reality of authentic experience, as opposed to generalities, theoretical models, and official pronouncements. In the army, it is what soldiers encounter on the ground, in a real battle or military operation; in organizations, people learn ground truth in their daily work and in the actual decisions made in organizations about solving problems, talking to customers, and handing out promotions, to name only a few. Some of the ground truths are about working practices; some are about values and norms. A substantial ethnographic report on organizational learning by the U.S. Department of Commerce estimated that at least 80 percent of learning happened informally on the job.[15]

Jean Lave and Etienne Wenger call the process by which newcomers simultaneously learn a group's practice and become a member of the group "legitimate peripheral participation."[16] Every word of that somewhat daunting phrase is important. When recognized as legitimate prospective members of a group (by virtue of their employment by the company and behavior that indicates they will probably fit in), the newcomers are more than just observers or visitors; unlike casual visitors or senior managers on tours of inspection, they can be let in on its "trade secrets." At the same time, they are onlookers at this early stage, peripheral to the critical work, their job being as much to watch and learn as to do. In effect, they learn by osmosis. Finally, they do participate both as observers and actors; they see how things are really done instead of relying on the more removed and often inaccurate picture that formal training provides. The group simultaneously teaches and tests the new recruit, using the process of showing him the ropes to judge whether he has the necessary qualities and abilities to become a trusted, productive member of the group.

By participating in the organization, the newcomer discovers its actual norms and values, which may not match its reputation, claims, or official policies. As Harvard psychologist Chris Argyris points out, an organization's espoused theory of action often differs from what he calls its theory-in-use.[17] We recognize the need to put espoused values to the test of reality in a host of clichés: where the rubber meets the road, actions speak louder than words, walking the walk. People are often surprised when espoused theory and theory-in-use coincide. So, for instance, a longtime recruiter at Russell Reynolds Associates says:

> When a new person joins the firm, they hear about our cooperative environment, but they don't believe it's real until it happens. They're always surprised when other members of the firm help them. With few exceptions, people will drop what they're doing when you ask for help. Here, help is offered before it's requested.[18]

Understanding and adopting organizational norms, values, and aims is an essential part of becoming a connected and productive member of an organization. As we have said, one important influence on the success of that assimilation is a predisposition to those values and norms: hence the importance of the hiring process. Another is for the recruit to see and experience them in action. When a newcomer learns firsthand that people really do comply with certain values and ways of doing things, he is likely to follow suit. And when a particular behavior becomes a genuine norm, the ever present social pressure of how "everybody" does things around here reinforces conformity.

PRACTICES

Everyone who has ever worked in an organization has seen the gap between official descriptions of how things work and how they really happen—the gap between what the manual says and what people really do. Sometimes hypocrisy or self-delusion lie behind the difference. More often, the complex and changing realities of work mean that it cannot be fully defined or understood from a distance. The "lived experience" of an organization or the work of a particular group can only be known by being there. The valuable knowledge and practice of how things really get done reside in networks and communities. Julian Orr talks about how Xerox's printer repair manuals solve only the simplest problems, and notes "the technicians' assumptions that their skills are not learned in school but from each other, and that the meaning of their talk about their skills is not obvious outside the context in which they were developed."[19]

The technicians, like people in many jobs, resort to what we call "unspeakable practices," methods unrecognized and sometimes unsanctioned by the official organization. According to Orr,

> *The work done by the technicians I studied is often very different from the methods specified by their management in the machine documentation. There is clearly a disparity between the tasks that they are told to accomplish and the means that are said to be adequate to the task. The technicians choose to give accomplishing the task priority over use of the prescribed means, and so they resolve problems in the field any way they can, apparently believing that management really wants accomplishment more than strict observation of the prescriptions for work.*[20]

Practices may be unspeakable in two ways. They may be so subtle, tacit, and context-dependent that they literally cannot be captured in words, and certainly not in words separated from the experiential understanding of the group that does the work. These are the practices learned through observation, apprenticeship, and the experience that gives people a "feel" for situations. Sometimes practices are unspeakable because they do not match official practices that are cumbersome or that mandate standardized behavior in unstandard situations. So, for instance, the Xerox technicians solve problems heuristically, "any way they can," and share their actual methods with each other but not with the organization's hierarchy. And most people in large companies have heard people say things like, "You're supposed to get six signatures on that equipment request, but if you need it right away, Joe can take care of it."

Or take this true story. A day or two after sending its check to the Internal Revenue Service, a small company discovered that it had made a huge error calculating the tax it owed. It had paid several times more than the actual tax due, a big enough difference to the organization's cash on hand to affect its performance. Company leaders made a frantic call to the IRS to request the return of the check. The IRS official told them that this was impossible—no mechanism existed to return checks; the extra money would be credited to them and would offset later payments. A secretary in the firm spoke up, saying she knew a woman who worked in that particular IRS office. Maybe she should give her a call. She reached her acquaintance and explained the problem. That woman quickly discovered that the check had not yet been processed; it was still sitting on someone's desk. She stuck it in an envelope and sent it back. It is harder to imagine a clearer example of the power of a personal network to cut through red tape with a simple, though unspeakable practice.[21]

INFORMATION DISTRIBUTION

Anyone who has ever worked in an organization of any size understands the role of networks as effective information conduits. Most interesting and valuable news comes from people close to you, either physically or because you work on a shared task, and from the members of your news networks. Who doesn't remember hearing through their networks about a key promotion, a joint-venture rumor, or a decline in revenue long before any official announcement was made? We recently asked four colleagues in four different large organizations to list six important decisions their organizations took in the past year and how and when they first heard about them. In every case they heard the news informally first through a phone call or e-mail from someone in their networks. This phenomenon may not be as important with respect to official announcements as it is to information tied to the local agendas of network participants.

In fact, a great deal of what is sent via e-mail today can be classified as "informal news." E-mail supplements and in some cases virtually replaces the phone calls that used to keep news networks up to date. This is one reason that people complain about e-mail overload and the hassles of answering so many messages, but they seldom disconnect from those sources. In a volatile world, we hunger for news, especially about our own organizations, and especially from true and trusted sources—our fellow network members. Complaints about receiving 200 to 300 e-mail messages in a day are usually tinged with pride because they attest to an individual's wealth of connections, his network strength—to being "in the loop." The people who receive only five e-mails rarely confess or celebrate their freedom from the burden of too much connection.

Networks carry more than news. They also provide information critical to work. When the research division of Bristol-Myers Squibb decided to analyze the varied degrees of success of their scientists in different clinical domains, they found that those who worked in BMS's oncology division had been unusually successful for quite a long time. The key difference between them and others in the firm was the richness, interactivity, and span of their networks outside the organization. The numbers of people inside and outside BMS who belonged to these oncology networks was substantially higher than network membership in other divisions, as was the total amount of communication and, where it was possible to measure, the density of connection—that is, the richness of content, meaning, and passion that flowed through those connections. This network-intensive way of working went a long way in explaining the group's outstanding performance.

KNOWLEDGE

The answer to the strategically important question "Where is the knowledge of the firm?" is that it exists, first and foremost, in the firm's networks and communities. This is true for several reasons. Knowledge tends to be local, sticky, and contextual.[22] It is difficult to codify, since so much of it remains tacit—embodied in people, visible in routines and activities, undocumented, and often (despite the claims of some) undocumentable. When people come together to accomplish work, they bring their varied tacit skills, assumptions, worldviews, and knowledge to the collaboration. As they work together, knowledge slowly moves from person to person, each absorbing and contributing to the dynamic mix, discussing, negotiating, and adjusting until some temporary equilibrium is achieved: "Yes, let's agree to do it this way." Through a similar kind of repeated communication and negotiation, knowledge is diffused through networks, and even sometimes through networks of networks.[23]

Even the best-designed intranet sites and knowledge repositories cannot replace these human knowledge networks. In a recent article on social network analysis, our colleagues Rob Cross, Andrew Parker, and Stephen Borgatti of Boston College's Carroll School of Management cite one study—now a couple of decades old—that finds people roughly five times more likely to approach friends or colleagues for information than use a database or other repository.[24] Their own research with about forty managers in a consulting firm reveals that 85 percent claimed to receive knowledge critical to the successful completion of an important project from other people. These managers routinely use the organization's knowledge base, but often only to supplement what they have acquired from other people—despite the fact that their organization has a leading-edge technical platform and institutionalized practices for capturing, screening, and archiving codified knowledge."[25]

The World Bank offers an excellent example of how networks both enhance information flow and function as knowledge repositories. Over the past few years, the Bank has organized over 100 "thematic groups," geographically dispersed networks devoted to specific practices.[26] Themes include water infrastructure, urban poor, rural transportation, and even social capital. About 50 percent of the World Bank's staff are active members of one of the groups, which vary in size from 40 to 700 participants. Each group has a modest budget for network activities such as meetings and developing technologies, and each has some specific roles attached to it—knowledge coordinator is one. Because the networks are organized by theme and the Bank has the necessary social and technical infrastructure, they help network members quickly locate the expertise or documents they need.

Here is one example. On August 20, 1998, the government of Pakistan asked the World Bank field office in that country for information on highway technology. The government said, "Our highways are falling apart and we can't afford to maintain them. We're thinking about using a particular new technology and would like your advice about it urgently." The team leader in the local field office sent an e-mail to the World Bank's network of highway experts saying, "I don't know about this highway technology and I need help in two days." The responses quickly came back: "Someone in Jordan has been trying it out; here's their experience." "Someone in Argentina is writing a book on the subject." The South African highway authority—a World Bank client—also responded, saying, "Here's our experience with similar technology." Within days, the field office in Pakistan had received detailed information and analysis about the proposed highway technology and was able to give the Pakistani government the advice it needed to guide its decision.

Appropriate communications technology communicated the question and carried the answers, but the technology was used only because the idea of a reciprocal network had taken root. Before theme groups were sanctioned, created, and supported, Bank team leaders and officials would have been extremely reluctant to admit their ignorance and inability to solve a problem to a sizable group of other employees. The fact that the Bank's reorganization into theme groups had the full support of the Bank's senior management legitimized the networked approach and made it possible to develop new behaviors that help employees do their individual work. In fact, it partly redefined work as group work. The social capital of both employees and the institution increased.

Once the process of communication and mutual aid within networks begins to be established, cross-network cooperation occurs too, as when a World Bank economist in Saudi Arabia sent a request to the Bank's Environmental and Socially Sustainable Development (ESSD) help desk for information on training related to operating air-quality-monitoring stations. The help desk immediately contacted an employee in Pollution Management who referred the help desk to someone in the South Africa region. After conferring with the Bank's training department, this person could inform the ESSD help desk person that although the Bank did not offer appropriate courses, the U.S. Environmental Protection Agency did. Catalogs were sent to Saudi Arabia.

COLLABORATION

Networks are incubators of collaboration, especially voluntary collaboration that does not rely on external incentives to spur it. A look at how service firms try to encourage participation in collaborative intellectual capital systems throws light on this process and its social capital implications. We have attended many meetings that try to deal with the issue of how to change behavior, especially around sharing knowledge (either in person or through documents). At the beginning of the knowledge movement, some practitioners thought that small, tangible rewards could spur individuals to contribute to so-called knowledge systems. They believed that rewards ranging from frequent flyer miles to mousepads to Dove Bars would convince busy professionals to write, record, or in some way document what they had learned on a project or assignment and so share their learning with others. Not surprisingly, little treats failed again and again. Not only did they insult the people who were supposed to respond to them, they made the whole knowledge effort seem fatuous. Some firms then tried to substitute the stick for the carrot by requiring employees to reveal how and what knowledge they shared, to whom, and when. This approach proved only somewhat more effective. First of all, it tried to compel people to share knowledge that was hidden in their heads and could only really be identified and disclosed voluntarily. Second, it suffered from what social scientists call "uncertain causality"; that is, the difficulty of determining exactly who developed/created, codified, diffused, or presented a "chunk" of knowledge made it difficult to apportion praise and blame fairly.

Continual, strong, direct leadership direction can probably make people share knowledge. According to Steve Kerr, GE's chief learning officer, when CEO Jack Welch is told of an innovative new process or practice at GE, his first comment is something like, "Great! Now who else have you told about this?" "No one," is not an acceptable answer.[27]

Not all firms are GE and not all leaders are Jack Welch, however. A better solution is the sharing that takes place naturally within networks, without recourse to artificial or juvenile measures, without carrots or sticks. Collaboration happens for several reasons.

For one thing, most organizational networks have norms of behavior they enforce by ostracism. Uncooperative, opportunistic people are isolated and in effect cease to be network members. Also, networks, like families, often provide "havens in a heartless world"—a refuge for friendship, membership, and identity, a place where everyone knows your name and the internal competition that limits cooperation is less evident. One *wants* to adhere to the network norms to fit in, to be a full member, especially if the accepted behavior is generalized reciprocity. On days when you have more messages than you can answer, whose do you choose to respond to and why?

Because networks and communities help create and sustain our personal identities, the intrinsic satisfactions of praise, respect, and gratitude from fellow members has more meaning and power than little prizes or even monetary rewards. The Xerox copier technicians who contribute tips to the Eureka database they share refused the company's offer of financial rewards because they felt payment would trivialize the more important rewards they got from helping and recognizing one another.

The Underside of Networks and Communities

We seem to have fallen into the familiar trap of talking about networks and communities almost entirely in positive terms. As we suggested earlier, though, the very cohesion of mutual commitment to a community can be a problem if that makes it clannish, insular, excessively idiosyncratic, or, in extreme cases, corrupt or destructive. The same kind of social connections that give people purpose, satisfaction, and a sense of identity are responsible for feuds and a sad history of violence against "them"—the outsiders. These networks also lock people out of jobs, clubs, and communities that any reasonable standard of equality would entitle them to participate in. One difficult task facing organizations and society as a whole is to understand how to maintain social capital, with all of its essential benefits, but reduce the clannish ignorance and hatred that sometimes accompanies (and even defines) being part of a group.

A form of this problem common in organizations—not a moral problem but still a problem for the organizations—is communities so wrapped up in doing "their own thing" that their work may not be of any productive use to the organization. This can be a delicate issue. Most of the valuable creativity in organizations comes out of communities *because* their members support each other in exploring what interests them. Too much insistence on having them think more about the organization may destroy their creativity. Aligning communities with organizational purpose without destroying their uniqueness is an important organizational challenge. John Seely Brown and Paul Duguid argue that the tension between community *practices* and the organizational *processes* that coordinate them for productivity and profitability can only be balanced, never resolved.[28]

Sometimes, too, an entire organization becomes so cohesive that it can be made rigid by a kind of "groupthink"—self-reinforcing beliefs that maintain a firm hold on the organization until the outside world proves them wrong—usually when it is too late for the organization to recover from its errors.

In general terms, the answer to these problems is to make the boundary defining the group more permeable—to let more people and information enter in from outside the group. Organizations that hire for cultural fit typically take care to hire some people who are different enough from the norm to challenge it somewhat. When communities need to work together, conversations at the boundaries between them are also places where a group's accepted ideas are often tested. Creating those connecting points is worth organizational attention. The network and community investments we discuss here are concerned both with increasing cohesion and broadening communities. Both goals are important.

Investing in Networks and Communities

Reams of research and the direct experience of almost everyone who has worked in an organization substantiate the value and importance of networks for knowledge and information sharing, collaboration, and job satisfaction. Yet we still hear of organizations that cancel travel and meeting budgets at the first sign of a profit downturn, when they should be investing more in their internal and external networks. They seem unaware that it is the depth, durability, and longevity of these networks that have made them so effective in the past and offer the best chance of renewed success.

Some organizations damage networks by heavy-handed attempts to overmanage them or by actions that impede their natural development. One of the authors attended a three-day meeting of all the partners of a Big Five consulting firm. Every hour of those days was scheduled and structured, with presentations and programs following each other from morning till night. Meeting organizers had provided so much "content" that there was no time for informal meetings and discussions—no time for "networking." Everyone we spoke to at the end of the meeting was exhausted and had obviously absorbed very little of the official wisdom being dispensed. Most distressing, though, was the palpable frustration felt by the participants who saw colleagues, friends, and acquaintances across the meeting tables and were desperate to have a chat with them. This was especially true for those whose previous discussions had only been via e-mail or phone and who were particularly anxious to talk face-to-face. The cost of lost opportunities was huge, yet no one openly challenged the format. One way to foster networks, certainly, is to give people time and opportunities to connect with one another. If the network is sound, the content is likely to take care of itself.

Sometimes organizations discover the existence of valuable networks inadvertently. Not long ago, IBM decided to make the various processes that go into developing corporate strategy more efficient and effective. At first, the focus was quite reasonably on those who worked in corporate strategy. Soon, however, it became clear to the internal consultants doing the work that essential people had been left out—people with diverse jobs throughout the firm, who were nevertheless part of the network involved in IBM's strategy processes. The project group grew from fourteen people to over seventy.

AVENTIS: A NETWORK INTERVENTION

Joe Horvath, another colleague of ours, and several other IBM researchers and consultants have been working with Aventis Pharma, a large European pharmaceutical firm, to encourage the growth of a new community to improve performance (and enhance social capital). The work started with a specific issue: Like every large drug firm, Aventis Pharma spends a great deal of R&D money seeking to develop new drugs for common illnesses. The costs are huge, but a successful new product can earn immense profits for the company. Any improvement in research capabilities has the potential to pay enormous dividends. Aventis found that it had drug development groups in New Jersey and Germany with a strong focus on immunology. But even though these groups were internally cohesive and dense, with internal ties for knowledge sharing and advice, little interaction took place between them. Aventis management believed that connections between the groups could be fruitful for both, and for the company. They believed that the greater the number of experienced scientists who looked at a problem—and looked at it together—the greater the likelihood the problem would be solved quickly and with more creative novelty. They asked Horvath and his colleagues to analyze the current situation and suggest remedies.

Standard consulting methods would probably have generated a familiar set of abstractions—boxes, models, matrices, and arrows—with a strong dose of technology as part of the answer. Horvath's group and several innovation-minded Aventis executives decided to focus on how the scientists solved problems in practice—where and how they sought the knowledge they needed and how they used their own network's knowledge base. Horvath had previously done work at Yale for the U.S. Army's project on working with tacit knowledge and was familiar with the concept of ground truth. Applying those lessons to the scientists proved fruitful: The work was done from the perspective of the scientist "in the trenches," not from any organizational idea about how work should be done.

They used extensive interviews, questionnaires, and observation to confirm that little interaction occurred between the groups and that what contact did happen focused more on sharing data and reusable models than on developing innovative solutions. Network analysis also revealed how individual network roles had developed and, most importantly, which individuals would be the best candidates for helping to develop a single community. Aventis also carried out benchmarking studies which led them to believe that similar situations were common in the pharmaceutical industry, so progress they made could give them a substantial advantage in developing new products.

Aventis Pharma management admitted to being dismayed by the lack of contact documented in the network analysis. They accepted the proposals Horvath and his colleagues made for encouraging a new, larger community to form. One recommendation was for a two-day meeting of key members of both groups to launch the new community. The fact that it was well attended, with busy scientists from both groups taking time to meet one another face-to-face, was itself a victory and a promising sign that the participants accepted the value of joining forces. The knowledge management program office began working in concert with the Information Services organization to provide technical support—another promising sign. With the help of human resources, incentives for community participation were added to official performance measures. Aventis believes that new ties are forming, building the new community. The consultants plan to "take the temperature" of the new group later in 2000, measuring usage of communication channels, relating that usage to problem solutions, and carrying out another network analysis—an "after" picture to compare with the dismaying "before" picture that convinced the company to act. As with any intervention to nourish the growth of organic social ties, the effort focused on connecting the right people and providing just enough technical support and formal incentives.

SOCIAL NETWORK ANALYSIS

Invented by sociologists and further refined by more mathematically-minded academics, network analysis tools look beyond formal organizational structures and peel away social poses to reveal the fundamental shapes and functions of networks. The more accurate picture they present can help network participants and managers improve network performance or make networks more robust or extensive. Often enough, the most effective interventions are modest: a new configuration of teams that helps bring isolated groups together, some communication tools, a little money, some face-to-face meetings. We have seen the way a small budget to fund semiannual meetings for a geographically dispersed network in a consulting firm created a new rush of energy and commitment and a strong sense of legitimacy. Members explicitly stated that entropy would have weakened their network without the meetings. Sensible interventions of this kind work best when network analysis provides a clear picture of the network strengths you are trying to reinforce and the problems you want to solve.

Network analysis also helps identify particular players who help (and occasionally hinder) the network. Certain roles recur with remarkable frequency and managers can provide incentives or mentoring to people in the valuable roles, or can look for individuals to fill them. There are *coordinators*, or *connectors*, often outgoing and friendly, who expend time and energy making connections among network members. Some people are *boundary-spanners*, who by temperament like spreading the news about who knows what to different groups outside the network, and often outside the organization. There are *mavens*, who cultivate specific expertise relevant to the network's tasks or operations and who are recognized as such by others.[29] There are *evangelists*—in a sense, fired-up boundary spanners—who trumpet the "good news" about new ideas, people, and processes in the network, generating enthusiasm in others. There are *gatekeepers*, who act as semipermeable membranes between networks and the outside world, regulating the flow of information that enters and leaves.

Network analysis also provides new insight into how knowledge moves in organizations. Although it is now well known that knowledge is mainly developed and distributed in networks and communities, most texts on organizational behavior assume that knowledge is somehow dispersed symmetrically, flowing equally to all members at the same time. While no member of a large organization believes this, no realistic model of knowledge dispersal is yet available. Network analysis is well on the way to providing one.

Along with some academic colleagues, our IKM colleague Rob Cross performed a network study of about forty managers in a consulting services organization. The analysis sought to clarify the key dimensions that made networks effective for members and the organization. The study identified four characteristics that powerfully affected the ability of people to draw on the expertise of others. Only when all four are sufficiently present do useful connections exist. Not surprisingly, all but one of these critical dimensions have to do with social capital issues of trust and mutuality, not just with questions of who knows what. The four dimensions are:

Knowledge. How well do people know what others know? How strong and well-founded are network members' reputations for having relevant up-to-date knowledge?

Access. Since time is a scarce resource in knowledge-intensive environments, getting access to the people who have knowledge can be difficult. In their study, Cross and his groups found that senior consultants and their considerable knowledge were often unavailable to others in the network.

Engagement. Engagement means actively listening to an inquirer, working with that person and his problem to provide genuinely useful knowledge and advice, not just a quick "dump" of information. A sense of connection with the other person and the issue is more valuable than knowing a lot.

Safety. Even in networks, which are relatively flat and nonhierarchical, people are sensitive to nuances of power and position and to issues of individual reliability. Before seeking knowledge, network members need to feel safe that their admissions of ignorance and need will not be used against them.

Cross and his colleagues also recently studied 114 managers in a large bank that had grown substantially by acquisition. Not surprisingly, management communications became an issue, since the networks of the newly joined organizations were not integrated. Research revealed that these sets of managers did not know what useful knowledge members of the other group had, were unsure whether they really had access to them, and had had neither time nor the repeated interactions that establish trust. This analysis proved helpful to the firm's executives who, not surprisingly, had given the issue little thought in the heat of acquisition. Ways to improve the situation are not hard to envision or carry out. For instance, strategically placing key network operatives so that they could diffuse their own network membership among new colleagues may be effective.

COMMUNITY ANALYSIS

To the extent that organizations want to focus specifically on communities of practice, the kind of network analysis described above can give clues to their shape and location. Multiple network connections among a group of people can signal the communication that happens within a community. Further inquiry can indicate whether those people exhibit other characteristics of a community of practice: involvement in a common endeavor, shared ways of doing things together, and what Wenger calls "mutually defining identities," among other indicators.[30] Researcher Eric Lesser and others at the Institute for Knowledge Management have developed questionnaires to help identify communities by looking for, for instance, informal meetings, common sets of work practices, documents, manuals, or databases that they use in common.

Again, leaders should avoid the simplistic notion that communities are automatically good, and that identifying and developing as many as possible necessarily benefits an organization. The existence of many emergent communities does provide some indication of the level of social capital in an organization, but it makes sense to focus community analysis on communities whose shared skill and knowledge are most important to the success of the organization. Etienne Wenger suggests that organizations identify strategically important competencies and then search for communities that "own" those competencies.[31] Interviewing known individual experts in those areas can help determine whether they are part of a community or a network of colleagues that can develop into one. Wenger cites interviewing processes developed by Shell and Chevron which do exactly that.

INVESTING WISELY

As these examples suggest, awareness and assessment are the first and in some ways the wisest investments that can be made in networks and communities. Applying the principle of "First do no harm" requires that you understand where valuable networks and communities are and what holds them together.

Through most of the 1980s, Chrysler was organized into functional departments: emissions systems, body, steering, electrical systems, and so forth. One group after another participated in the design of a new car, passing on its work to the next in line.[32] At the end of the decade, the company began to reorganize around car "platforms," or model types, instead of functions; those new groups included engineers in all the areas needed to produce a new car design. By most measures, the reorganization succeeded brilliantly, reducing design time by 25 percent and developing cars with more customer appeal than older models. Disturbingly, though, defects began cropping up in the new designs, many of them problems that had been successfully solved in the past. The company seemed to be forgetting some of what it knew about designing cars. Damage to components of social capital turned out to be the source of this organizational amnesia. The disbanded functional departments had been rich communities of relationships through which experienced engineers shared what they knew and trained and mentored new-comers. Successful in most ways, the reorganization that broke those departments into smaller groups disrupted important com-munities of practice, and problems resulted. The company did not know the communities were there, performing essential knowl-edge sharing, until they disappeared.

To some extent, the very fact of doing an assessment and indi-cating awareness and interest can help networks thrive. The fol-lowing are some judicious actions that leaders can take to encourage networks to develop in ways that benefit the organization.

Money. Providing enough funding to support face-to-face meetings, buy collaborative technology, free up a key individual's time for more network activity, or perhaps hire an outside facilitator can aid networks. Too much money can distort networks, however, training members to behave as they think their funders want them to and so losing some of their natural ways of working.[33]

Space. Networks need space to grow, bond, and expand. That space is sometimes physical and sometimes cyberspace or cog-nitive or social space. The learning and trust that develop in net-works is dependent on appropriate and sufficient space.

Recognition. We all need encouragement. Many organizations are remarkably bad at offering it, as if managers feel that giving praise is a sign of weakness. Many networks live and die, bringing value to organizations, without ever being recognized for what they do. A little recognition can improve morale and legitimatize network activity.

The Network-Building Organization

We have suggested here the value of networks and communities—their contribution to learning and knowledge exchange, collaboration, membership, and commitment, and the intrinsic rewards of belonging and being appreciated. Their centrality to social capital and its benefits can hardly be exaggerated. Social capital lives mainly in these networks and communities. We have suggested some of the ways organizations can understand and nurture those webs of connection. These investments matter, because people live and work in networks. Some firms spend freely to recruit talented employees only to find out much later that these people never connect with internal networks and are substantially underused. In some cases, it becomes apparent that the prior performance of the newly hired "star" depended as much on the network he belonged to as on his own abilities. In other cases, senior people hired away from firms carry much of their network with them, decimating one company and enriching another.

Several prominent theorists believe that network-centrism will be *the* guiding principle of successful organizations in the near future, since networks so powerfully create and manage knowledge, enforce social norms, encourage commitment, and create more democratic workplaces. Time will tell. We have no doubt that networks are critical to organizational social capital and that investing in network vitality grows social capital.

We emphasize again the importance of nurturing existing organic structures and encouraging voluntary connection over trying to mandate community and cooperation. The World Bank's Steve Denning, instrumental in the development of that institution's thematic groups, says that the most successful communities were those built on groups that existed informally before the corporate initiative began, their members drawn together by shared passion for their subject.[34]

In the next two chapters, we look at the most basic contributors to the connections that bind networks and communities—that make them what they are. Chapter 4 argues for the importance of giving people in organizations the space and time to spend together so that they can build the trust and mutuality upon which networks and communities depend. Chapter 5 considers the conversations and stories that help create the ties that bind, the words and gestures we use to understand one another and to forge social connections in cultures and organizations.

4

❖

SPACE AND TIME
TO CONNECT

All good things take time to develop.
—LEWIS MUMFORD

IN 1998 Alcoa moved its Pittsburgh, Pennsylvania, central office
staff from a thirty-one-story tower built in the fifties to a new,
six-floor headquarters designed to connect people with one
another. Open offices, glass-walled conference rooms, and a six-
story atrium allow employees to see many of their colleagues at
work. People move from floor to floor on escalators, not hidden
in elevators, as they were in the old building. Unlike office buildings
whose ducts, plumbing, elevators, and stairwells occupy a central
core that diverts foot traffic and blocks sight lines, the Alcoa building's "service core" lies to one side, leaving the heart of the building free for work and connection. Family-style kitchens near the
center of each floor of offices encourage workers to mix and chat.[1]

Alcoa CEO Paul O'Neill, who championed the move and the
new headquarters, sees the design of the new workplace as integral to his goal of increasing collaboration, connection, and interdependence. He worked closely with the architects to eliminate
traditional elements that isolate people and devise areas that are

"magnets for collaboration," in the words of architect Martin Powell. O'Neill contrasts the social impacts of the old and new buildings:

> *In the old building I would drive into the garage, get on the elevator right by the entry door and go upstairs. I'd run into three people on the elevator and that's how many people I saw each day—except for those I had scheduled appointments with. Now if I have something to do on the first floor, lunch or whatever, I take the escalator down and I see 50 people or 50 people can see me. It demystifies the notion that CEOs are royalty or something who don't have anything to do with real people. There's a sense of connection.*[2]

As O'Neill suggests, the design of the new building helps narrow the gap between bosses and employees in the process of making it easier for people to meet and talk. Because everyone uses the kitchens, open spaces, and escalators for the same purposes of eating, meeting, or moving around the facility, those facilities tend to be socially leveling. Old-style executive dining rooms reinforced difference and distance—that is part of their purpose. These public spaces contribute not only to accessibility but to a kind of equality. O'Neill intensified the sense of solidarity by making senior managers guinea pigs for the new open workplace. Almost three years before the move, he had the top floor of the old building gutted and put senior executives and their assistants in open offices there, with a communal kitchen at the center. O'Neill's office in the new headquarters is the same nine-by-nine-foot cubicle that everyone else has. He explains, "The size of my cubicle says to the rest of the organization that they are as important as I am as measured by their workspace. That's what it ought to be to get the organization to work together."[3]

Alcoa's new headquarters is an investment in social capital. Making the life of the workplace visible, providing places for people to meet and talk informally, and expressing the commonality of workers at all levels in the design of the offices all help cultivate the trust, connection, and perceived equity that mean high social capital. Places to gather, to meet, to talk, to see and be seen, and time to do those things, are essential ingredients of social capital. Leaders who want to build social capital in their organizations would be wise to invest in social space and social time.

Of course, providing a space for it no more guarantees sociability than e-mail guarantees knowledge sharing. The infrastructure fallacy—if you build it, they will use it—applies to building design as well as to technology. We spoke to one professor who cannot remember once having a casual "stairway conversation" with a colleague during the several years he had an office in a graduate school building designed to encourage serendipitous contact. Social space and social time are part of the indivisible matrix of social capital supports. They will succeed where trust and collaboration flourish, and will reinforce those norms.

The Power of Place

Social relationships flourish in social spaces. For thousands of years, people around the world have gathered in town squares, commons, cafés, pubs, restaurants, and parks, in marketplaces, post offices, and general stores. In those places they connect and reconnect, exchanging gossip and advice, celebrating and commiserating together. They form and strengthen the ties that bind them into communities. They build trust and understanding; they shape and recalibrate reputations. Athenians met in the agora twenty-five centuries ago to buy goods, but also to hear what was going on, renew relationships, and define their collective identity. In fact, the word *agora*, though usually translated as "marketplace," more literally means "the gathering place." People in rural American communities meet in the local café or general store for the same purposes. When such places disappear or people lose the habit of frequenting them, community is hard to come by. As Ray Oldenburg remarks in *The Great Good Place*, without "the core settings of informal public life" such as piazzas, cafés, and pubs, "even the native does not feel at home."[4]

Look at the so-called bedroom communities outside major cities in the United States, most of whose inhabitants work in the city or at offices in other suburbs. We know the ones near Boston best, but the pattern repeats itself again and again: subdivisions of single-family homes, many separated from neighbors by a half acre or more of lawn, few sidewalks, "downtown" areas consisting mainly of strip malls strung along a main road. Recently, the leaders of some of these towns have tried to strengthen the sense of community by installing clock towers or fountains with benches and walkways nearby to provide a focal point for gathering. Whether or not these efforts succeed, they at least recognize the importance of physical centers of gravity to draw people into relationships with one another and with the places they live. Towns that have real centers—in New England, often complete with greens or commons—command a substantial premium in real estate prices.

Some new planned communities—Disney's Celebration has gotten the most publicity—have been designed with community-building spaces specifically in mind. Sidewalks and front porches encourage people to see one another and meet and mingle, the garages that seem to dominate so many contemporary homes banished to service roads in the rear. Plazas and parks abound. These communities raise some still-unanswered questions. Commentators have asked whether their somewhat nostalgic designs represent missed opportunities to reimagine what contemporary communal environments should look like. There is also the issue of whether they may be excessively planned and controlled and therefore lose some of the spontaneity and naturalness that contribute to authentic connection. Again, though, Celebration recognizes and celebrates the important connection between community spaces and community.

The lack of attention to these issues in most organizations until recently probably reflects at least two factors: failure to understand the role of community in the organization and a striving for economy and efficiency based on a narrowly utilitarian definition of work. Organizations sometimes only see the true usefulness of cafés and libraries when they eliminate them. In *Grooming, Gossip, and the Evolution of Language*, Robin Dunbar recounts the experience of a TV production unit that had productivity and morale problems after being moved to a new "purpose-built" workplace:

> It was some time before [company leaders] worked out what the problem was. It turned out that, when the architects were designing the new building, they decided that the coffee room where everyone ate their sandwiches at lunch time was an unnecessary luxury and so dispensed with it. The logic seemed to be that if people were encouraged to eat their sandwiches at their desks, then they were more likely to get on with their work and less likely to idle time away. And with that, they inadvertently destroyed the intimate social networks that empowered the whole organization.[5]

The architects who eliminated the coffee room and the leaders who approved their plans did not set out to destroy community. They simply failed to grasp its productive value or even its existence. They incorrectly assumed that work only happens when people are alone at their desks. With no real understanding of the social dimensions of work or the relation between community and place, they could not know how essential those apparently "idle" conversations in that "unproductive" space were until they took them away.

HOTELING: WHERE NOBODY KNOWS YOUR NAME

The arguments for "hoteling" are also about economics and efficiency and similarly ignore the value of relationships shaped by regular opportunities to meet. Why maintain expensive offices for consultants and others who seldom use them, the thinking goes. If 50 percent of your workforce is on the road 60 percent of the time, providing individual offices for everyone wastes money. Instead, some organizations maintain generic offices that individuals can reserve and use when they need them. All are equipped with desks, phones, and access to office support, so it should not matter which particular office an individual uses on any particular occasion. The problem, of course, is that hoteling dramatically reduces opportunities to get to know others in the organization. When individuals use offices infrequently and are surrounded by a different set of "colleagues" when they do, they cannot develop the kinds of connections that form when people spend time together. And these "rented" offices lack the pictures, memorabilia, and furniture arrangements that help express one's office identity. Like guests at hotels, employees without permanent offices are usually isolated in generically anonymous surroundings. "People in hotels strike no roots," notes Edward Verrall Lucas. "The French phrase for chronic hotel guests even says so: they are called dwellers *sur la branche.*"[6]

If connection, community, and a sense of membership are organizational goals, leaving employees out on the branch is not a good idea. Companies that calculate the financial benefits of hoteling should also count the social costs. And they should take an honest look at how consistently they apply the practice. In some Big Five consulting/accounting firms, nonpartners are forced to "hotel," but partners generally keep their own offices. This of course sends strong signals about the desirability of private space as well as lessons on power and privilege.

In *The Social Life of Information*, John Seely Brown and Paul Duguid describe an unsuccessful experiment in space management at Chiat/Day, the advertising company, which shows the failure of a kind of hoteling. Chiat/Day management mandated "hot desking" for its employees, thinking that making any desk available to anyone—first come, first served—would generate new creative energy. Employees hated the plan. Groups that needed to work together could not do so from randomly scattered desks; people wanted a place for personal items. So they subverted the system. Among other acts of rebellion, members of teams came to the office early to lay claim to groups of desks that, in theory, could not be reserved. When new owners took over the company, they dropped the practice.[7]

Space for Social Capital

The knowledge management conversation of the past few years has begun to focus attention on the importance of meeting places to the development and use of organizational knowledge. That discussion has emphasized knowledge exchange, and especially the serendipitous sharing of ideas between people who could not have guessed that one knew something the other needed to know. We want to make two social capital points about those knowledge spaces, many of them cafés, alcoves, and other communal areas designed to encourage chance meetings and casual conversations.

One is that knowledge exchange depends on social connection. Without some degree of mutuality and trust, the knowledge conversations will not get started; without some degree of shared understanding, they will not go very far. The libraries and cafés and stairwells where people meet only work as knowledge incubators when levels of social capital are reasonably high. The related second point is that the knowledge exchanged in those meetings is often social knowledge—shared aims and interests discovered, signals and stories shared that build confidence, trust, and connection—rather than technical or business knowledge that can be directly applied to a product or problem. These spaces breed social capital, strengthening and expanding the relationships that shape networks and communities. They earn their keep as social capital invest-ments—sources of new and strengthened relationships—even when no obviously valuable new ideas or solutions to problems arise. So the knowledge-exchange spaces that have begun to appear in firms recently are also social capital spaces.

Social spaces are likely to work best when they harmonize with people's natural social habits. Putting spaces where people already gather or walk makes more sense than hoping a special conversa-tion area will attract them. So, for instance, when Lars Kolink, the CEO of Oticon, the hearing-aid firm, noticed that people who met each other on the stairways often stood and talked together, he had the office space rebuilt to create broad stairwell landings with coffee machines and places to sit that would encourage them to extend those conversations at the places they naturally occurred. In fact many organizations—Alcoa among them—pay special atten-tion to how people move around the building, recognizing that those movements present natural opportunities to bring them together. As with Alcoa, many organizations now design their offices around escalators or central open stairways where people can see one another, rather than the small boxes of elevators that move them invisibly from floor to floor. The Lowe and Partners advertising firm in New York describes its three-story central stair-case as "the communal heart" of the agency.

One social truth is that people mainly interact with those in close proximity and those they see carrying out their normal work-day itinerary. A recent study by British Telecom found that work-ers on different floors of the same building typically had only a 1 percent chance of meeting one another on any given day. Awareness of that social truth led Viant CEO Bob Gett to insist that each of Viant's offices occupy only a single floor. As the business grows, Gett's organization launches a new office rather than expand to other floors and exceed a maximum of 200 employees in any one office. Open offices for everyone, including senior managers, increase opportunities to exchange ideas and build trust relation-ships. The open offices let everyone know what is going on, even what the CEO's phone calls are about.

Instead of criticizing its engineers for their apparent reluctance to exchange information with one another, Corning designed a new engineering building to complement the ways they do connect. The company asked Thomas J. Allen, then a professor at the MIT/Sloan School of Management, to study the actual behavior of the hundreds of engineers who would work in the new building. He concluded that more than 80 percent of their ideas arise from face-to-face contact with each other *and* that they are willing to walk only about a hundred feet from their own desks to talk to anyone else. In keeping with those findings, the William C. Decker Engineering Building includes twelve discussion areas with coffee machines and wall-size blackboards so that at least one will be in every engineer's immediate "neighborhood." Again, open stairs, escalators, and ramps connect the building's three floors to increase the ease and naturalness of contacts.[8]

New Takes on Traditional Spaces

Some organizations, consciously thinking in terms of community building and not just knowledge exchange, have begun to model their meeting spaces on traditional communal spaces from outside the corporate world. Some of these, such as the kitchens at Alcoa and the living-room-style sitting areas at Boeing's St. Louis leadership center, duplicate domestic spaces. Viant's open offices cluster around the focal point of a central kitchen and "play area" with a pool table and video games.

Some firms try to humanize larger offices and build community by modeling spaces on the main streets, town squares, and neighborhoods of traditional communities. So, for instance, designers took a "city planning" approach to the Northern Telecom world headquarters in Toronto, dividing it into neighborhoods whose inhabitants help design their own environments, creating some of the variety that evolves naturally in a city as a reflection of the different characters and behaviors of the groups that live there. Main streets and side streets connect these areas; street signs point the way to particular destinations and encourage exploration.

The f/X Networks office in the Fox Tower in Los Angeles borrows the idea of the small town post office to bring people together. Rather than have mail delivered to desks or picked up from a traditional (and traditionally unattractive) mailroom back near the loading docks, designers created a central post office where employees go to get mail and refreshments and, if they choose, continue conversations and hold informal meetings in the adjacent open spaces.

Waterside, the British Airways headquarters in London, completed in 1998, consists of six buildings arranged along a central covered street where trees and fountains along with a library, café, bank, supermarket, and restaurant draw people to the shared main thoroughfare of the complex. Bridges, glass-walled elevators, and open stairwells give people a view of this public area as they move through the facility. This not only increases the chances that people will find someone they want to talk to; it helps make the collective life of the organization visible. It shows that the organization *has* a collective life, a fact that the elevators and mazes of walls and cubicles of a high-rise building can strip of its reality.

These environments promote walking and talking, two activities that Oldenburg recognizes as being important to community life: "In walking, people become part of their terrain; they meet others; they become custodians of their neighborhoods. In talking, people get to know one another; they find and create their common interests and realize the collective abilities essential to community and democracy."[9] The social value of these places does not depend entirely or continuously on meeting and talking. Even seeing and being seen by other members of the organization creates value. Watching the public life of the organization and taking part in it simply by being there contribute to the sense of community. In a speech about the benefits of city parks he gave more than a century ago, Frederick Law Olmsted, architect of New York's Central Park and much of Boston's park system, described "each individual adding by his mere presence to the pleasure of all others, all helping to the greater happiness of each."[10] At first glance, this may seem an overly sunny view of massed humanity, but in fact it reflects the exhilaration and interest many of us feel being part of the crowd in a well-designed public space. Joining the commuters and visitors who pass through the recently renovated Grand Central Station in New York City or watching the chatting friends and families and children sailing toy boats in the Luxembourg Gardens in Paris on a sunny Sunday makes one, at least briefly, a participant in the life of those cities. In organizations too, the public spaces where people see and are seen by each other generate energy, connection, and a sense of belonging to a community of human beings, not an abstraction called "the company."

In many of these facilities, the geographic center is the heart of the communal space, the crossroads at which people naturally meet. Like Waterside and the Alcoa building, many new structures built with community in mind push the necessary machinery of elevator shafts, heating ducts, and other service hardware to the periphery and reserve the center for the social machinery of meeting rooms, atriums, kitchens, cafés, and open stairways or escalators.

Space as Symbol

We have discussed how cafés, lounges, main streets, libraries, and alcoves in stairwells attract people. They encourage and extend conversations; they let people see each other. Along with those practical purposes, they have symbolic value. When the chairman of Oticon had the stairwells of the company's offices redesigned to give people places to meet and talk, he proved that he valued these casual conversations and considered them essential to the future success of the firm. Oticon's investment in them sanctioned and encouraged an activity employees might have thought (or thought that their managers thought) was a time-wasting escape from real work. Informal meeting places signal organizations' belief in the value of informal meetings (though, as we warn, other, stronger get-back-to-work messages can drown that signal out). In conjunction with other consistent signals, they embody the company's commitment to social connection, providing not just social spaces but permission to socialize.

Some graduate school facilities built in the last decade or so—the Kennedy School of Government, the Haas School at the University of California at Berkeley, and Boston University's School of Management, among them—attest to their schools' belief in the value of connection in the atriums that increase the chances of seeing and meeting colleagues and fellow students. BU's John Henderson remembers that supporters of the open design had to stand up to some who objected to spending money on "empty space." Shad Hall at Harvard Business School offers a counterexample. It conspicuously lacks meeting rooms and gathering places, and testifies to the proposition that every professor is an island, entire unto himself (or herself), and that collaboration is neither expected nor invited.

The transparency of office spaces such as those at Steelcase, described in our discussion of trust, also has both utilitarian and symbolic value. Transparency means you can see what others are doing and more easily know who is engaged in work related to yours. It also signals commitment to openness. Open offices for the CEO or CFO and conference rooms with glass walls symbolize an organization in which people have nothing to hide, where they trust each other and work interdependently. Those physically transparent spaces literally create organizational transparency: open access to information about what the organization is doing.

Where particular spaces are located has symbolic importance too. A hard-to-reach lounge at the edge of a facility both literally and figuratively marginalizes the gatherings that might occur there. At Unipart, the resource center of the corporate university is at the heart of the firm, next to the reception area of the group headquarters building.[11] That placement tells employees and customers that the "U" matters to the organization. The central location of kitchens and meeting spaces at Alcoa, Viant, and other organizations, and the main street at British Airway's Waterside not only make meeting more convenient, they demonstrate and symbolize the central importance of those places.

As we have already suggested, executive floors, executive dining rooms, and "mahogany rows" also function symbolically. They signal separation between leaders and employees, between us and them. They flatly contradict official statements about the openness of the organization, about meritocracy and the breaking down of hierarchies, and about community. Office design linked to status is about separation and difference by definition: that is what status means. The advertising slogan of the 1950s, "A name on the door, a Bigelow on the floor," left no doubt that the right kind of carpet—along with the biggest windows and the mahogany desk—signaled success and power. Even now, in the age of cubicles and a growing interest in open planning, the old status/space equation has not disappeared. Large firms still employ tape-measure wielding "space police" who make sure that no employee has more square footage than his level entitles him to. Only a few years ago, one of the authors was denied permission to put a small conference table in his office because he had not reached the appropriate level in the firm he then worked for. The problem was resolved when the facilities director ruled that a scratched top and wobbly legs sufficiently offset the hierarchical value of an old table discovered in storage.

The intimidation caused by the impressive office and its executive secretary gatekeeper is sometimes a deliberate and sometimes an incidental by-product of the office as reward, or an assumed need for privacy. Alcoa chairman Paul O'Neill, who insists on occupying the same nine-by-nine-foot cubicle that everyone else in the company's headquarters uses, describes the effect of the lavish office he occupied in a previous job: "My former Washington office was the kind of space that intimidated people. . . . I had to work hard to let them know they shouldn't be. For certain things, there's something nice about that kind of place. But for an organization trying to create human connections to make things go forward, it almost kills real communication and creates an artificial environment."[12]

Physical space can also communicate messages of continuity and tradition. Developing plans for a new Malden Mills factory to replace the one destroyed by fire, architects Bechtel, Frank and Erickson and Malden Mills CEO Aaron Feuerstein chose to shape the new building around the only surviving part of the earlier structure: an Italianate brick tower that contained staircases and elevators. They had considered demolishing the tower or moving it from its location near the center of the site, but eventually decided that the remnant of the old factory forged an important link to the past, a visible assurance that the new Malden Mills would hold on to the values of the old one. At the same time, the awkwardly placed tower forced the architects to interrupt the shape of the massive building, giving it a more human scale that itself suggests the company's human values. In some ways, the choice to preserve the tower despite the practical difficulties it presented parallels Feuerstein's decision to hold on to his experienced workforce by paying them while the factory was being rebuilt.

MEETING IN CYBERSPACE

Online "chat rooms," "team rooms," "communities," "bulletin boards," "forums," "town meetings," and "agoras" use the language of traditional meeting places to describe multiparticipant exchanges, implying that they are functionally equivalent to really being there. We consider that vocabulary misleading and wishful. Professor Sim Sitkin of Duke University asks whether cyberspace can create a genuine sense of *place*, with the texture and particularity that that word implies, rather than an abstract and dimensionless *space* in which people exchange messages.[13] We will take up the complicated and mixed story of "meeting" in cyberspace in more detail in chapter 7, but we can say with reasonable certainty here that cyberspace cannot adequately substitute for "real" places. The clearest weaknesses of meeting in cyberspace (at least given the current state of technology) are:

- a much narrower range of communication, with gestures, facial expressions, feelings, and tones of voice vastly reduced or missing;

- a weaker sense of participating by observing (unlike the silent members of a physical group, individuals who monitor an online discussion without contributing to it tend to disappear);

- fewer opportunities for serendipity, the unexpected sights and sounds that fill physical meeting places and tend to get filtered out of cyberspaces devoted to specific themes or tasks.

We believe that virtual meetings work best as part of a mix of kinds of contact (whether you think of face-to-face meetings and work as cementing e-relationships, or e-mail as maintaining relationships that originated through face-to-face meetings). Most relationships *based* on e-mail lack the depth, resilience, and trust that effective networks and communities require. In some cases, reliance on e-mail can reduce social capital among people at the same location. When everyone in the workplace spends most of the day focused on his or her computer screen and when people get in the habit of e-mailing their neighbors instead of visiting them, then important opportunities to connect and communicate are lost. The lure of cyberspace—the shifting scene on their computer monitors—can mentally remove people from the real space they occupy; their thoughts are elsewhere, as the saying goes.

Time: The Final Frontier

The battle for adequate social space has not been definitively won. The single-minded pursuit of efficiency still drives organizations to eliminate gathering places they consider superfluous or even detrimental—

tempting people away from "real" work they should be doing at their computers and desks. Nevertheless, the word on space has been getting out. Many leaders now recognize the value of meeting places and invest in them. Oticon, Alcoa, British Airways, and Viant are among thousands of firms that include cafés, atriums, town squares, main streets, and conversation nooks in their office designs to obtain the benefits of knowledge exchange and social connection, and to offer workers an appealing environment—attractive cafés, homey kitchens, and courtyards are "weapons" in today's war for talent.

The battle for time is tougher. Even leaders convinced of the value of social time in organizations find it nearly impossible to act on that belief. For many people, the twenty-four-hour-a-day global economy, lean organizations, expectations of instant response, and—ironically—new communication technology seem to have made "slack time" a thing of the past.

Speed matters, but not at the expense of everything else. In addition to damaging social capital, speed can limit the basic thoughtfulness that complex work requires. The "zero response time" that *Fast Company* identifies as an organizational goal only makes sense when rote responses will do. A standard response can meet a routine demand, but few demands are routine these days. The idolatry of speed can tempt organizations to do poor work quickly. A former employee of Digital Equipment Corporation has said about that company's troubled period, "We didn't know what we were doing, but we sure did it fast."[14] And physicians some-times talk about "SSW" diagnoses: swift, sure, and wrong.

The managers of many organizations seem to regard time to talk and get together as an unaffordable luxury, but we believe that this apparent luxury is in fact a necessity, an essential social capital investment. Building relationships takes time. We are not talking about large chunks of free time or even about time away from work—trust relationships develop in the course of working together—but relationships and networks need some time—some breathing space—to grow. "Time escalates commitment to relation-ships" into "highly valued, trusted relations," notes Denise Rousseau.[15] And ethnologist Patrick Bateson says, "As familiarity grows, individuals come to sense the reliability of each other."[16] Trust, understanding, commitment, and the habit of reciprocity develop over time. There is no such thing as instant social capital.

Even a modest investment in social time can pay off. Look again at United Parcel Service, a firm as concerned about efficiency as any, but not at the expense of relationships among employees and between employees and customers. What follows is how one of the authors learned about the UPS approach to the issue.

WORKING LUNCHES

Around two o'clock most afternoons, three or four chocolate brown UPS delivery vehicles park together near a small park in this suburban town northwest of Boston. In good weather, the drivers (wearing uniforms the same familiar brown as their vehicles) sit on a couple of the benches at one edge of the park. Some days a stack of packages rests on the sidewalk near one of the vans while they eat lunch and talk.

Having seen them there three or four times when I drove by, I finally felt compelled to stop. I introduced myself and explained my reason for intruding. They glanced at each other—it must have seemed odd, a stranger asking them what they did during their lunch hour—but they answered my questions willingly enough.

Yes, they got together to have some company at lunch, but "We talk about everything and anything," including a lot about work. For one thing, they solved problems of how to get hard-to-deliver packages to their recipients. Drivers who had worked in town longest could tell newer drivers how to find unmarked streets and addresses and when particular customers were likely to be available to sign for a delivery. The veterans shared other special knowledge too: which customers wanted packages left in the garage or around the side of a house; when school let out and there were kids to watch for on the street and busses slowing traffic.

I pointed at the half-a-dozen cartons stacked on the sidewalk near the benches. Why were they there?

"If one of us has more packages than he can deliver and someone else has a lighter day, we can move things around so all the deliveries get made."

"Or if there's been a missort at the Center, we fix that."

"Sometimes one of the guys needs to finish early, so you'll make some of his deliveries. He'll do the same for you another day."

So they made midday adjustments at these lunch meetings,

responding to unexpected circumstances that arose during the morning's work, taking stock of what still needed to be done. I asked if these daily meetings were sanctioned by company management or if they were completely informal, an unacknowledged and unofficial part of the workday.

"Our supervisor knows we meet here," one of them told me. "If he wants to talk to us together, he'll show up."

Other conversations with people at all levels of United Parcel Service made it clear that this kind of informal meeting happens daily in most places. Thousands of drivers gather in parks, coffee shops, and parking lots around the country, socializing, helping each other out with information, sometimes exchanging packages or otherwise sharing the work. Industrial engineering experts at the company look for the tiniest efficiency gains. As we mentioned in Chapter 1, the "340 methods" drivers learn describe the most efficient ways to carry out every aspect of their work in painstaking detail. No one watches the drivers to make sure they comply, but most adopt such practices because they help them get their work done. Getting packages delivered on time is the bottom line for UPS. Even so, the drivers and the company see the value in these lunchtime meetings, which take some drivers away from their routes and must seem inefficient from a purely industrial engineering point of view. Contrast the lunchtime practice of UPS drivers with the sandwich-at-the-desk quickly swallowed by so many harried office workers. Not having time for a shared meal with colleagues increases the isolation of a day's work in the cubicle.

Every day too, UPS drivers and distribution center managers gather for a three-minute prework communication meeting (or PCM) to make announcements and deliver a safety tip, but also as a kind of prework huddle, a team gathering before the drivers go off to their individual routes. The efficiency-conscious company calculates the cost of these meetings down to the dollar, but willingly makes the investment. At some centers, the night shift of loaders overlaps the day shift of drivers so that they can get to know each other personally, building relationships that reinforce the loader's incentive to load the package cars correctly (the quality of the loading job has a direct major impact on the driver's ability to get his job done). These are all relatively modest but important investments in social time.

UPS also came to see the value of having its drivers spend some extra time with customers. CEO Jim Kelly says that management realized that the drive for efficiency made the company "a little rigid." They recommended that drivers spend an extra half-hour a day with customers.[17] The dozens or hundreds of brief contacts that drivers have with particular customers build robust relationships over time. These relationships produce valuable customer information and loyalty. They sometimes develop surprising depth; one driver who had the same route for several years reports being invited to three weddings of customers' children.

TIME TO GET CONNECTED

Some of the most important time investment is made during the first hours, days, and weeks that new employees spend in organizations—an investment that companies where new staff must "hit the ground running" refuse to make. But how can, say, a newly hired senior consultant who has not yet connected with colleagues and has only an outsider's knowledge of company norms and values represent the firm to a client? In contrast to organizations that expect this kind of instant productivity, driven by the pressure of client demands and the desire to get every possible dollar of revenue out of the new talent, some organizations invest in extensive orientation and training programs that help build personal networks and trust while they teach new hires "how things are done around here."

Even though it operates in the high-speed world of Internet commerce, Viant's leaders believe that it takes about seven months to weave new hires into the social fabric of the organization and teach them enough about how the company works to make them productive. They call this period "time to talent." Their three-week orientation program, mandatory for all new employees regardless of previous experience or the demand for their particular expertise, lies at the heart of the assimilation process. CEO Gett, who calls himself the company's chief cultural officer, believes that the intensive three-week experience creates social connections that will serve individuals throughout their Viant careers and gives newcomers a sense of membership and participation that helps bind them to the firm. The company's 9 percent turnover rate, unusually low in this volatile industry, suggests that he is right.

TIME TO STAY CONNECTED

Traditionally at Hewlett-Packard, employees have been encouraged to go early to meetings or discussions at other HP sites so they could walk around, meet people, talk to old acquaintances, and generally see what was going on. That extra few hours was an investment in social time and social connection.

Russell Reynolds Associates recruiters and researchers contend with the fast-paced executive search world. Clients seeking to fill critical senior positions want results "yesterday." Yet the organization consciously resists the temptation to respond instantly. Russell Reynolds Associates requires that recruiters embarking on a new search make five phone calls to people within the firm before they call any potential candidates or outside sources, to ensure that the search will not be too narrow—Russell Reynolds wants to find the best candidate, not a good-enough candidate. The "five-call rule" also reinforces social networks in the firm by making sure that busy recruiters take time to stay in contact with each other. Although focused on the new search, the calls reinforce relationships, let people in the firm know what each other is doing, and create opportunities for exchanges that go far beyond the particular search.

The weekly meetings held in every Russell Reynolds Associates office similarly combine direct contributions to specific searches with an opportunity to share experiences and reinforce the trust relationships that the company depends on for its effectiveness. It is not surprising that the firm invests time and effort in social gatherings for employees too. (One recruiter remarked that the company spends more time and effort building relationships within the company than it does on building relationships with customers.) These occasions are explicitly seen as opportunities for relationship-building within the company. Meeting organizers even dedicate attention to seating arrangements at dinners, pairing firm members who do not know each other well but are likely to benefit from a closer personal connection.

The Xerox supervisor who intentionally delayed the start of meetings of copier repair technicians to give them a chance to chat with one another was investing time in knowledge exchange and relationship building, though to some people his slowness in "getting down to business" probably seemed lax and inefficient. Former

IBM CEO John Akers, who told employees to stop wasting time at watercoolers and get back to their work, failed to understand, first of all, that the employees were working while they stood around together. They were discussing the company's problems and looking for solutions to them. Nor did he see that they needed time together to maintain the trust and social cohesion threatened by the layoffs and uncertainty caused by IBM's difficulties. It is easy enough to criticize his action in retrospect and think that savvy leaders would not make that kind of mistake today, but recent decisions by intelligent leaders facing tough times are not so different. As we write, we see several excellent companies slashing their travel and meeting budgets in response to lower-than-expected profits and falling stock prices. Perhaps today's market-driven economy creates irresistible pressure to cut that supposedly discretionary spending. In the long run, though, limiting people's opportunities to meet and talk will weaken the cooperation, mutual commitment, and group creativity that the long-term success of the firm depends on.

Investing in Space and Time

Space and time for people to gather and make connections with one another are the seedbed and sunlight of social capital. By providing them, leaders can foster conditions that help social capital thrive. If you want people to connect, to talk, to begin to understand and depend on one another, give them places and occasions for meeting, and enough time to develop networks and communities. Social capital needs breathing room—social space and time—within work and surrounding work.

Although we describe examples of intentional and sometimes expensive social spaces, not all organizational social spaces need to be carefully designed and designated main streets or town squares. Respecting existing "emergent" social spaces (like the coffee room in the TV production office Dunbar mentions, or the parking lots UPS drivers may meet in) is equally important. In fact, naturally occurring spaces can invite more authentic and comfortable connection than places that are too obviously designed to encourage conversation.

Nor do companies need to provide endless or aimless time for employees to "relate" to one another. Again, the UPS examples show that even brief connecting times in a day mainly driven by time-saving efficiency can be hugely important. On the other hand, trust relationships take time to build, even if that time consists of numerous short connections over a long period. Remember the discussions of "quality time" some years ago? The popular media briefly latched on to the idea that busy parents could make up for long absences from home by making sure that the limited time they spent with their children was fully engaged and rich with content and connection. It turned out, though, that relationships and efficiency do not mix well. The children were not always ready for meaningful togetherness exactly on schedule. Duration matters. Even speed-reading was never a particularly good idea. (In one of his films, Woody Allen brags about speed-reading *War and Peace*. "It's about Russia," he says.) Speed bonding and speed loving make even less sense. To some extent, quality time must be quantity time. Geoff Mulgan writes about what he calls "the economics of attachment," the need for sufficient time to form social connections: "All attachments and memberships take time, and time is scarce. We cannot be members of an infinite number of groups in the same way because attachments require not just "quality time" but also quantities of time, to learn about the people involved, their motivations and idiosyncrasies."[18]

These truths may be self-evident, or nearly so, but acknowledging them is easier than acting on them. Investments in space and time should go together, and sometimes they do. The firms that provide cafés, plazas, and meeting alcoves are more likely to give employees time to meet than those that do not, but the equation is by no means certain. We see offices where attractive and strategically placed café tables are never used, not only because people are too busy, but because sitting at them means risking censure: "Don't they have any work to do?" We need to enlarge our definition of work and moderate our passion for speed. Building connections, trust, and a culture of collaboration *is* valuable work, and it does not happen without available space and time.

Many discussions of meeting space and time—including ours, to some extent—say little or nothing about what people talk about and how they communicate when they get together. Most commentators mention "knowledge exchange" or "social talk" and leave it at that. But what people say to one another and how they say it matters a great deal to an organization's social capital. So we devote our next chapter to a closer look at communication and especially to the social art of storytelling.

5

❖

SOCIAL TALK AND STORYTELLING

Good, the more communicated, more abundant grows.
—JOHN MILTON

IT IS NEAR THE END of a long day in an unfamiliar city. A team of half a dozen people, drawn, as it happens, from two offices of a software company, has spent ten hours trying to get a new system up and running at a client's headquarters. They have faced some familiar problems (familiar to most of them; the youngest of the six is on his first assignment). The installation took longer than expected, so the trainer had to use a CD-ROM simulation rather than the live system; the client company's president had to fly to a regional office to deal with a problem and postponed the "kickoff" speech; and the head of IT had somehow got the idea that the system already had a feature that in fact won't be available for six months.

The six sit in the hotel lounge, drinks in front of them, a silent TV flashing news pictures over the bar. They swap some travel stories—"my worst flight"—and joke a little about whose idea it was to pick a restaurant with singing waiters, but mostly they talk about what went well and badly that day. The trainer says, "About the fifth time I said, 'If we had the system running . . .' they started to laugh, so I told myself, 'Shut up about the live system.'" They talk about how upset the IT guy was, and one says, "We need to tell marketing not to oversell this stuff—again."

The conversation turns to other, worse disasters. One veteran tells the story of the time the team arrived at the offices of a major client and discovered that all the software and equipment had been lost in transit. "Always carry everything with you," he tells the new guy, whose participation in the discussion has been mainly through listening. "I don't care how heavy it is or who promises to get it there, carry it yourself."

Later on—they're all tired but keyed up too, reluctant to go off to bed—they start talking about some things going on in the company: "How did *he* get promoted?" asks one. "He looks great from a distance," another answers, "but I don't think he's going to last." The conversation drifts to why-I-joined-the-company stories and experiences at school. Two of the technicians, who have known each other for over a year, discover that they were both turned on to computers by middle school science teachers. One says, "Mine told me, 'You're a nerd—make the most of it.'" They all laugh. Soon they head for their rooms—all but the two technicians, who decide to have one last drink together.

Social Talk

That familiar scene offers an example—several kinds of examples—of social talk, and suggest some of its absolutely central importance to building and maintaining social capital. Telling and listening to stories, chatting, sharing a little gossip, are the main ways that people in organizations come to trust and understand one another. Of course, coworkers share a lot of technical expertise in such conversations. When peers in any profession get together, they invariably "talk shop," and often enrich their knowledge doing so. But as importantly, they also share social knowledge and build social ties. Conversation and story are the voice of social capital. They communicate values, behaviors, understandings, and aims—all the shared cultural messages that define groups and turn individuals into members of groups. Also, a conversation or a story is itself a social act: the simple fact of sharing one makes or strengthens a connection.

Some years ago, *Fast Company* cofounder Allan Webber gave several talks on the theme of "Start Talking and Get to Work!" He especially emphasized knowledge sharing, but much of the important knowledge shared is social knowledge. What the talkers build is not just a stock of expertise but a stock of social capital.

INFORMATION SHARING VERSUS COMMUNICATION

You might think that we talk to one another more than enough. This seems to be the golden age of communication. Cellphones, faxes, pagers, e-mail, and videoconferencing keep us in constant touch with one another. Television, radio, and the Internet give access to endless information about the world, billions of messages about everything from sports scores to weather reports to histories of Egypt to theories about the origin of the universe to instructions for assembling a bookshelf to medical breakthroughs to conspiracy theories to the mission statements of ten thousand corporations to where a particular movie star had dinner last night and what she ate. Even a list of all the subjects mentioned on the World Wide Web would be overwhelmingly long and various, touching on almost everything people think and talk about. We seem well on the way to total connection. "We are becoming a grid, a circuitry around the earth," said Lewis Thomas a quarter of a century ago.[1] The circuitry has clearly thickened and expanded since then. H. G. Wells's earlier prophecy of a "giant brain" girdling the earth seems a distinct possibility today.

At the same time, though, cultural commentators worry about isolation, anomie, and decreasing social capital. Robert Putnam's *Bowling Alone* documents a decline in the habit of association among Americans and a parallel loss in community awareness, mutuality, and trust; other observers detect diminishing civility, a word that suggests not just politeness but behaviors based on recognition of commonality, a common stake in society.[2] Somehow the connected world is also the fragmented world. It is not at all clear that our greater ability to send messages to one another increases social capital as much as we might think, or at all.

When the God of the Old Testament decided to put a stop to humanity's first great collective enterprise, he confused their language so they could no longer understand one another, and their ability to carry out the joint project of building the Tower of Babel disappeared. Certainly, losing the ability to understand a coworker asking for help carrying a heavy stone creates a problem, but that kind of request could probably be made without words. The real problem was the damaging loss of understanding that cannot be mimed or diagrammed: without common speech, the tower's planners could not have inspired others to join the project, workers could not have learned to trust each other's judgment, resolve unexpected problems together, or count on each other's help in dangerous situations; they would have had no way to encourage each other, teach each other, or figure out what to do about the guy who sneaks off for a drink, or share their frustrations and satisfactions about the job.

In other words, the failure of social talk (and loss of social capital) was probably more critical than the failure of information exchange. Our current obsession with information—and with keeping up with the latest information—may lead people to assume that exchanging news bulletins is the same as being connected or that it makes other kinds of connection unnecessary. Not so. Too much emphasis on information can get in the way of real connection. John L. Locke puts it this way:

> Our personal voices began to fade. The seeds were sown when tiny tribes of humans gave way to large and diverse cultures that had fewer pieces of shared information and a greater need to exchange impersonal facts. The process continued when we developed quicker ways to transmit messages and to conduct economic and personal business. Our appetite for information exploded when improved travel and mass communication multiplied the number of things we need to know about to compete and feel safe.[3]

As a result, he says later, "Intimate talking has been edged out by news bulletins. Our sentences are increasingly swollen with facts. Spontaneity has taken a plunge. The emotional warmth has gone out of speech."[4] The problem is not just too much information, but information driving out social talk, or conversation.

THE ART OF CONVERSATION

Conversation binds communities and builds social capital. Geoff Mulgan asserts that "the most elementary [social] unit is arguably not the family, but rather the conversation."[5] And, as Oxford cultural historian Theodore Zeldin asserted in his BBC talks on the subject, conversation "involves more than sending and receiving information."[6] Conversation includes gossip, stories, the mutual discovery of meanings, the negotiation of norms and aims, expressions of sympathy and disapproval, bewilderment and understanding. It implies mutuality and a kind of engagement or relationship. "I had a conversation with the person sitting next to me on the plane" means that you went beyond comments about the food or your reasons for traveling and got to know each other a little, discovering subjects of mutual interest or shared values. It also means that you both talked, though some conversations do tend to decline into monologues. Zeldin remarks, "There can be no satisfactory conversation without mutual respect."[7]

Conversation includes tone of voice as well as words, and nonverbal expressions when conversation occurs face-to-face, as many real conversations do. Conversations are rich in tacit and explicit content, as E. M. Forster's description of a man who couldn't "get conversation" suggests: "He never noticed the lights and shades that existed in the greyest conversation; the finger-posts, the milestones, the collisions, the illimitable views."[8] Go to your local café and watch people at the other tables. Even if you cannot hear what they say, you can watch their conversations. The listener nods or frowns or looks away; the pair or trio move closer together or further apart as they talk. One may be distracted by something else going on in the café (by your observing him, for instance); one may glance quickly at his watch—that familiar, hard-to-hide gesture of impatience or lack of interest. A continual stream of silent conversation accompanies the spoken words, tacitly relaying such statements as, "Do you agree?" "I understand." "I don't know what you're talking about." "I'm thinking about something else and only pretending to listen." "My turn now." "I admire you." "I love you." "Yes." "No." "I don't believe you." "I can't wait to get out of here."

The reaction of a group of deaf people watching Richard Nixon's famous I-am-not-a-crook speech on TV shows how much nonverbal communication communicates. The group laughed all the way through Nixon's earnest talk because his dissembling showed so clearly in every gesture and facial expression. Undistracted by the sound of his words, they literally saw what he was really saying.

This complex give and take, the interaction and mutual work of creating a conversation, is how people understand one another They need to engage in real conversation, with its rich flow of messages and subtle negotiation, before they can really understand. Sending a memo or making a statement does not create this level of understanding, or the social capital that depends on it. According to Alan Mulally, director of engineering for Boeing's 777 project,

> [T]he biggest problem with communication is the illusion that it has occurred. We think when we express ourselves that, because we generally understand what we think, the person that we're expressing it to understands in the same way. Well, in my experience I've found that's very difficult. When you're creating something, you have to recognize that it's the interaction that will allow everybody to come to a fundamental understanding.[9]

John Seely Brown of Xerox similarly recognizes that understanding depends on interaction, conversation carried on over time to build mutual respect and genuine understanding (rather than assuming that because something has been spoken, the people who hear it understand). Brown describes a nine-month process of regular meetings between Xerox PARC researchers and engineers to build shared understanding of a new technology. Without those conversations, the two groups were a bit like workers at the Tower of Babel, speaking different languages, but with the added problem of seeming to speak the same one—often using the same words to express very different assumptions.

We emphasize conversation rather than information sharing to assert the importance of conversational give-and-take in building trust and connection for cooperative work. Question and response, explanation, argument and assent, redefinition, repetition, and nonverbal signals—the whole gamut of conversational resources—contribute to the mutual understanding and respect that joint commitment to collaboration requires. To put it another way, conversation builds social capital in ways that information sharing does not.

The Xerox meetings and the interaction that Alan Mulally talks about are examples of conversation about work. Their focus is the task at hand but their openness, mutuality, and duration create understanding and social connection among the people involved. (What we said in the last chapter applies here: adequate time for social talk is essential.) Social talk not directly tied to work also has value for organizations. This is even true of gossip, part of the conversational repertoire of social groups.

Two Cheers for Gossip

Even outside the workplace, gossip has a bad reputation. We think of gossip as mainly about the failings, foibles, and misfortunes of others, and there is some truth to that negative emphasis, though people gossip about success and good fortune and babies being born too. Still, we generally see gossip as petty, unreliable, intrusive (sticking your nose in other people's business) and sneaky (talking behind someone's back). At work, gossip is considered all these things and a waste of time besides. These complaints reflect some truth; gossip can be malicious and harmful. We endorse it here, in a qualified way, because it also serves important social and organizational functions. Gossip is one way groups assert and agree on their values and behaviors. In criticizing someone for taking credit for a colleague's work or using flattery to win a promotion or calling in sick on sunny Fridays, the gossips imply shared beliefs about the right way to behave. As John Locke adds, "although group members gossip for the pleasure, in doing so they negotiate community norms and identify themselves with those norms."[10] They also negotiate agreements about who is trustworthy, talented, and hardworking and who is not. Gossip helps devise an annotated map of communities and networks, telling people where they should and shouldn't turn when they need help, keeping tabs on the reputations that define the social structure: Nicholas Emler, a psychologist at Oxford University, has also been particularly interested in gossip and its uses. After listening in to conversations in Scotland while he was based at Dundee University, he too came up with a figure of about 60 to 70 percent devoted to social topics. (He concluded that one of the most important things gossip allows you to do is keep track of—and of course influence—other people's reputations as well as your own. Gossip, in his view, is all about the management of reputation.)[11]

We talked earlier about the importance of reputation, that barometer of trustworthiness which determines whether someone will be ignored or confided in, ostracized or sought after. Gossip shapes and communicates reputation.

Gossip is also about belonging. It asserts relationship. We gossip within the groups we are members of about the people we know (putting aside the complex pseudorelationships implied by gossip about movie stars and other public figures). Says John L. Locke, "The reason gossip is enjoyable—actually the reason it's possible—is that all the participants know the individuals whose actions and reputations are under review. If Penelope Eckert is correct, people may even need to belong to a group just 'to know how to gossip in it and to be allowed to.'"[12]

It makes sense that the word *gossip* derives in part from *sib*, meaning close relation, as in *sibling*. Gossip is intimate. It reflects and increases people's sense of membership. Gossip about the company as a whole—will it be sold? Why is that new product late? Why was *he* promoted?—is insider activity, a part of belonging and involvement.

Gossip is one element of the mixed and far-ranging kind of conversation that John Seely Brown and Paul Duguid call "chat" in *The Social Life of Information*.[13] Like *gossip*, the word *chat* has negative connotations, suggesting pointless, superficial talk. In fact the very looseness of chat gives it value, situating information about work in a social context of reputation, relationships, and values, opening the door to expressions of the intuitive understandings that people use to get real work done as well as "hard facts" that so rarely explain what to do in unexpected situations. Brown and Duguid describe the Xerox tech reps' habit of getting together for breakfast or lunch or at the end of the day to gossip, eat, play cribbage, and talk about work all at once. Rather than being pointless or unfocused, this informal mixture is especially powerful. Synergy exists between the seamlessly blended social talk and work talk; they support and enrich each other. The social ties validate the work knowledge and ensure nuanced mutual understanding; the work knowledge strengthens social ties. Brown and Duguid say, "Chat continuously but almost imperceptibly adjusts a group's collective knowledge and individual members' awareness of each other." Much of the value of chat comes from not being too purposeful. Rather than zeroing in on a particular issue, it goes where it goes, discovering important insights at the end of unpromising paths, simultaneously building connections between ideas and connections between people. Chat invites conversational serendipity that can create unexpected value.

How Organizations Support Conversation

We are not suggesting that organizational leaders encourage employees to gossip. Most of us need no encouragement. We do urge them to recognize the power and legitimacy of social talk—gossip, chat, and story—and to encourage informal conversation in a number of ways:

- by providing social spaces for people to meet in (and authorize conversation by doing so);

- by allowing time to talk;

- by favoring face-to-face conversation;

- by broadening their definition of useful talk to include chat.

The companies whose investments in social space we described earlier have demonstrated a recognition that conversation goes beyond information exchange. Some of these investments are justified in terms of knowledge sharing, but many of the organizational champions of meeting spaces talk specifically about encouraging the social conversation that makes that sharing possible. They have incorporated in their facilities exactly the kinds of communal spaces where conversation happens; those kitchens, cafés, main streets, and parks invite wide-ranging social talk rather than narrow focus on the task at hand.

Conversational companies like UPS and Hewlett-Packard frequently favor face-to-face meetings and develop various ways to support them in addition to providing some good talking spaces. For instance, the leaders of Hewlett-Packard have long encouraged "managing by walking around." David Packard explains that these direct connections between managers and the employees they supervise need to be "frequent, friendly, unfocused, and unscheduled—but far from pointless."[14] In other words, these are opportunities for conversation, not just information delivery or incidents of checking up on people. Packard says that the visits he and Hewlett made to HP facilities around the world always included opportunities to walk around "to meet and chat informally" with employees.

The Power of Stories

Stories have particular power to build and support social capital. For one thing, they convey the norms, values, attitudes, and behaviors that define social groups probably more fully—with more rounded context—than any other kind of communication. Portraying situations and events, they show by example. Listeners learn by "seeing" people in action in a story more effectively than they could from abstract tenets that are less memorable and more difficult to apply to real life. Equally important, shared knowledge of story events—what *happened* more than the lessons taken away from what happened—draws people together. For instance, although many Americans would probably call honesty an American ideal, it is our shared lore of George Washington confessing to chopping down the cherry tree that gives us common ground, more than the abstract idea of honesty. Meeting a person who knows as we do that the engine in *The Little Engine That Could* says, "I think I can" on his way up the mountain and "I thought I could" on the way down creates a kind of bond that meeting someone who admits to sharing our ideal of "perseverance" does not. And the act of telling and listening to a story is itself a social event. Like having a meal together or a drink at the pub, the experience of sharing a story connects people and helps define them as fellow members of a social group. And stories convey the personality of the teller, not just information about what she believes or has done. The novelist E. M. Forster described story as "the repository of a voice."[15]

The virtually universal human fascination with stories argues for their social importance. Go to your local bookstore and see how much shelf space fiction and biography occupy—in other words, how popular stories are. Flip through books in other categories—

business, psychology, politics—and note how often these books use stories to engage readers and get their points across. What percentage of self-help books strive to persuade their readers through stories of people who saved their marriages, gained confidence, lost weight, recovered their health, learned to say yes to life or no to unreasonable demands? Stories exist in every culture. For many thousands of years, social groups have told and retold their stories, sharing tales of who they are and what they believe, passing on their particular understanding of what it means to be human. From the *Iliad* and the *Odyssey* to the Bible to the Arthurian legends and the story of the Magna Carta to tales of the best salesman the company ever had to family stories of the time Uncle Jack rescued the dog from the fire (or maybe the dog rescued Uncle Jack), people define themselves as social groups through their stories. Their sense of membership comes both from the content of the stories and the fact that they all know them—possessing the same stories becomes a badge of membership. Some commentators concerned about what they perceive to be the fragmentation of American culture point to the decline of shared stories, even the stories that TV tells us, as one source and symbol of the problem. Once, "everyone" watched *The Ed Sullivan Show* or *I Love Lucy* or *All in the Family*. Now, with proliferating cable stations and TV shows targeted to particular audiences, even the shared experience of separately watching the latest episode and talking about it together at work the next day is less common. Only a sports event like the Superbowl and occasional dramatic news stories partly fill this gap.

Many people in and outside organizations believe that judgments and opinions should always be based on rigorously logical analysis—a belief in so-called fact-based decisions. Some think that information can explain everything. Experience suggests, however, that human beings make sense of themselves and their world mainly narratively. Sociological and management literature often depict decision making as a rational process of gathering and weighing information, but in real life, decisions are more often shaped by persuasive stories.

One of the authors worked for the Harvard Business School for a number of years and audited classes while he was there. The classes and the texts used in them were linear, logical, and analytical. They suggested that leaders made decisions by carefully weighing the pros and cons of various options to determine which offered the best balance of promise and risk. When he first worked as a consultant, he expected business to work that way, but it didn't. As he got involved in senior-level discussions, he noticed that stories, not analysis, usually carried the day. People would discuss and analyze data for a while, but then someone would say, "Well, let me tell you what happened four years ago when our market share dropped 14 percent in Germany." If anyone responded, it would be with a counterstory or maybe a story that supported the first one. Very rarely would anyone say, "Let's analyze that." People frame their thinking in stories; that's the way they bring human values, feeling, and conviction into the process; it's the way they bring social reality into a discussion of abstractions.

Many CEOs have storytelling skill, even if they are reluctant to call attention to it. It certainly comes to the fore when they meet with financial analysts and tell stories about the firm's future products. What else could they do but tell stories, since facts about the future are in short supply? Harvard Business School professor Christopher Bartlett says that Jack Welch of GE considers his Irish heritage, with its storytelling tradition, as a valuable asset. So it is not surprising that Howard Gardner's *Leading Minds* identifies storytelling ability as an important leadership skill.[16] The persuasive power of stories and their ability to meld knowledge, context, and feeling has made storytelling an important topic in organizational discussions. Conferences on storytelling in business are beginning to appear and attract attention. Storytelling is increasingly seen as an important tool for communicating explicit and especially tacit knowledge—not just information but know-how—the hard-to-capture assimilated understanding of how work gets done. And stories, we believe, are an essential social capital tool, preserving and transmitting the basic belief and nuances of culture, establishing reputation and building trust—and doing all that through storytelling occasions that are themselves important social activities.

What Is a Story?

Stories vary widely in length, style, complexity, and even how much they are explicitly presented as stories rather than slipped unannounced into the flow of conversation. (A distinction Steve

Denning of the World Bank labels "big S" and "little s" stories.[17])
Virtually all stories share basic elements, though. Each has one or
more main characters or protagonists who face an opportunity or
problem; it tells how the protagonist responded to that challenge
and what the outcome was—the success or failure of the effort and
perhaps what effect the experience had on the protagonist or on
others in the story. The story of Odysseus's ten-year-journey from
Troy back home to Ithaca and the story of the tech support person who finally figures out what the customer on the phone is
trying to say both fit this pattern.

Stories contain at least some circumstantial details of time, place,
appearance, or setting. How much of this kind of information they
have varies tremendously (from the spare narrative of biblical parables to the rich detail of novels by Dickens or Balzac), but some
description of what it was like to be there seems necessary to make
stories memorable and convincing. Circumstantial detail makes stories vivid and believable. In fact, plausible circumstantial detail often
persuades people of the truth of totally fictitious and basically
implausible urban legends (about alligators living in New York City
sewers, for instance) and now equally specious Internet legends.

What we can call "I-witness accounts" have a kind of built-in
plausibility that secondhand accounts do not. Of course the stories
are interpretations of events, not the events themselves, but "I was
there; this happened to me" are powerful claims to authenticity.
This is especially so if the teller has a reputation for reliability, but
the relationships between the reputation of the teller and the plausibility of the tale is interesting and complicated. Stories and their
tellers reciprocally vouch for each other. Yes, we are more likely to
believe a story told by someone we consider honest than someone
we have learned not to trust, so the reputation of the teller validates
the story. At the same time, stories validate or discredit their tellers.
The tone, internal consistency, plausibility, intelligence, and depth of
the story influence our impression of the speaker.

In other words, stories tell their tellers. They are not merely
reports on events; they reflect the values and beliefs of the people
who choose to tell them, and choose to tell them in just that way.
We use stories to explain, validate, and present ourselves to others.
This is why telling each other stories is one of the important rituals
of courtship. Simply being given access to details of another person's

life creates connection and intimacy, but these stories also reveal what the other person cares about, and how they see themselves and the world. What perhaps matters most is which among the millions of events in their lives they decide to talk about, and what attitudes their ways of narrating those events reveal. Though less romantic, the process of building social capital connections at work is also a kind of courtship, and storytelling plays a similar role in the process of discovering people and groups. Poet and essayist Wendell Berry asks about members of communities, "How can they know one another if they have forgotten or have never learned one another's stories? If they do not know one another's stories, how can they know whether or not to trust one another?"[18] Stories are basic to how we know and trust one another, and how groups create and maintain coherence.

Social psychologist Elliot Mishler's description of narratives as "identity performances" hits the mark. He says, "We express, display, make claims for who we are—and who we would like to be—in the stories we tell and how we tell them."[19] When we say, "Tell me your story," we are really saying, "Tell me who you are and what you think about life." And often we learn much more about the identities and values of people when they tell us what happened to them than we do from their descriptions of themselves or statements of belief. Similarly, stories of what happens in organizations tell more about them than their official pronouncements. These stories of organizational identity do much more than vision and mission statements to create the sense of membership and engagement that is part and parcel of high social capital. They help tie together individual identity and organizational identity. That is why Howard Gardner writes that *"stories of identity*—narratives that help individuals think about and feel who they are, where they come from, and where they are headed— constitute the single most powerful weapon in the leader's literary arsenal."[20] Rick Stone's Storywork Institute helps organizations become "self-knowing organizations" by collecting "identity stories" that capture their values and history. So, for instance, Nighttime Pediatrics of Salt Lake City brought Stone in because it feared that rapid growth was causing it to lose sight of its original mission and values. Stone gathered stories from staff into a book called *Nighttime Stories* that helps new employees understand the history, norms, values, and aims of the after-hours pediatric health care center. Stone also uses the book to help train leaders to develop their own storytelling skills and use them as a management tool.

We tell stories to know each other and to discover or create meaning. Stories select events out of the stream of experience and relate them to one another. As Brown and Duguid say, "Stories are good at presenting things sequentially (this happened, then that). They are also good for presenting them causally (this happened because of that)."[21] They make sense of things that may not have been at all clear at the time. Although stories are usually told from the beginning ("It all started when . . ."), they are constructed retrospectively. That is, the teller chooses a starting point and selects particular events and details in light of what happens later. Dozens or hundreds of other events that might have seemed just as significant or insignificant at the time are left out because they do not contribute to the result that defines and shapes the story. (See Jean-Paul Sartre's *Nausea* for a sense of what life feels like when stories lose their power.)

The ability of stories to make sense of events along with their ability to evoke the real-life feel of a situation and to illustrate rather than assert the values, norms, and feelings that motivate people gives them tremendous power to communicate the richness and texture of a culture. Hence the importance Wendell Berry and others give them as instruments of social coherence and their importance to social capital in organizations. Part of that power comes from the way listeners engage in or "relate to" stories, entering into them by putting themselves in the hero's place and perhaps reinterpreting the action in terms of their own experience and situations. A *Harvard Business Review* article describing 3M's preference for narrative strategic plans over bullet points, emphasizes the ability of stories to inspire and galvanize, to engage people. "When people can locate themselves in the story," the authors say, "their sense of commitment and involvement is enhanced."[22]

Stories engage listeners because a person—a hero—is at their center. We identify with the heroes of stories because each of us is the hero of our own story, trying to overcome the external and internal obstacles that stand between us and our goals. They also engage because they leave room for interpretation and reimagining. The point or moral of a story is not equal to the story itself. In fact, explaining a story can kill it, reducing story to statement. This is not to say that a story means whatever a listener chooses. If that were true, stories would have no power to pass on the values, thoughts, and feelings of cultures and organizations; they would not communicate. Academics who favor deconstructionism argue that this is exactly the case, but the experience of cultures and individuals over many thousands of years proves them wrong. Good stories are flexible and suggestive, they provide opportunities for interpretation and response, but only within a range of meaning the story establishes. The fact that they do not have one simple point does not imply that they can mean anything at all. An employee who interprets a story about the boss firing someone who questions his judgment to mean that the boss welcomes criticism will soon discover that deconstruction works better in theory than practice.

The power to engage and motivate gives stories advantages over more abstract forms of communication. Asked to develop a major knowledge management initiative at the World Bank, Steve Denning came face-to-face with the problem of communicating a new idea to a large, dispersed organization. Memos, charts, and models explaining the value of knowledge management had "zero effect," Denning says. No matter how carefully and intelligently composed they were, these abstract documents lacked the power to interest or engage people. One-on-one conversation did work, Denning adds, but there is no practical way to talk directly to everyone in a large, dispersed organization. He found that only storytelling combined the emotional and persuasive power of direct conversation with the reach of other forms of public communications.

Organizational Stories

Defining story types is tricky. It would be easy to multiply categories and talk about dignity stories, value stories, equity stories, stories of membership, inspirational stories, cautionary tales, knowledge stories; or to go in the direction of genre and discuss comic stories, serious stories, fables, and parables. We have chosen types that we believe have the most direct and powerful impact on organizational social capital, but admit that someone else might make a persuasive case for another list and that even the stories in our fairly broad categories shade into one another. That is in the nature of stories; the good ones say a lot and defy easy description.

ORGANIZATIONAL MYTHS

We sometimes think of myth as untrue, but we use the word here in another sense: to define a culture's fundamental stories, the ones that express its basic views of itself and the world, that explain what matters and how things work. Some myths describe events that actually occurred and some do not. Whether they are fact or fiction seems to have remarkably little connection with a myth's power to define and influence identity and behavior. The Greek myths that underlie the *Iliad* and *Odyssey* and those poems themselves express and help shape the Greek view of the world: from a belief in the uncertainty of the universe and of human behavior to Greek ideas of heroism and hospitality.

Organizational myths too help shape and define the organization. These stories of founders and early critical events and turning points remind members (and tell newcomers) what this place is all about: what it exists to accomplish; how things are done here; what people believe and value; how they relate to customers, competitors, and society at large.

A now familiar story from 3M that quickly became a defining organizational myth recounts the invention of the Post-it note. Briefly, it goes like this. Because he sang in his church choir, Art Fry saw the need for a way to mark pages in the hymnal that would not damage the book but would stay in place better than the slips of paper most people used. So he saw potential in an adhesive that 3M researcher Spence Silver had developed years before—one that did not stick very well but that Silver shopped around the company rather than consigning it to the rubbish heap of failed experiments, hoping someone would find a use for a weak adhesive. Fry believed enough in his idea to build a machine to make the sticky notes in his basement at home when he was told that the manufacturing process would be costly and complex, and then gave out samples at 3M when the marketing department claimed customers would not be interested in such a product. Of course, Post-it notes became a huge success for the company.[23]

What makes this story mythic, rather than simply a story of one organizational hero, is the way it embodies the essential 3M values and behaviors that define the company and also the way it recalls similar stories that date back to the firm's beginnings. Many decades earlier, company founders bought a mine that they believed would be a source of corundum, a valuable abrasive. When they discovered that they were wrong, they visited potential customers to discover what needs they had that might be met by products made from the lower-grade minerals the mine *did* contain. The Post-it note saga parallels this organizational "creation myth" in several ways. Both stories tell of going out into the field to discover an unrecognized need; both describe cases of turning an unpleasant surprise (the low-grade minerals, the adhesive that wouldn't stay stuck) into something new and useful. "When you get lemons, make lemonade" might be considered a company slogan. Both stories demonstrate persistence and initiative. (Individual initiative is institutionalized in 3M's 15 percent rule, which allows and encourages researchers to spend up to 15 percent of their time pursuing individual projects.)

Here is another company creation myth. One of the authors did some consulting with a firm called NEBS (New England Business Services), a successful manufacturer of business forms—in fact, a Fortune 500 company. Those familiar multicopy carbon paper receipt pads at the dry cleaner or gift shop are made by NEBS. At least fifteen of the twenty or so people he interviewed at the firm told the same story of the firm's origin. In the twenties, they said, the founder of the firm took his automobile to a garage for repairs. The owner of the shop ripped a piece off a brown paper bag hanging on a nail and wrote the cost of the repair on it and when it would be done. Being in the printing business, the founder saw an opportunity in this makeshift system of providing receipts. He devised standard forms to do the same thing better, and they were a great success. The familiar company story expressed a lot about how the employees thought of their work: the down-to-earth usefulness of their products, responsiveness to the need of customers, innovation based on common sense. As it happens, the story is untrue. It survives, though, and continues to work because it represents real truths about the organization; employees recognize themselves and their work in it. We might call this story a true lie. Although it did not happen, it expresses truth about the culture somewhat as the fictional *Huckleberry*

Finn expresses truth about America. Sometimes stories and legends that are not literally true tell a powerful truth about company culture and help explain it to newcomers and remind others of who and what they are. Similarly, by the way, some stories tell false truths. That is, they describe real but anomalous events that do not genuinely represent the organization.

Like the central myths of other cultures, from the Hebrews and Greeks to countless nations, tribes, and communities today, organizational myths contribute powerfully to social capital. They are a shared possession that draws people together, as the Greeks of Periclean Athens were drawn together by their joint "ownership" of Homer's great poems. They vividly represent values and behaviors that define the common culture, reminding old-timers who they are and what they believe in and teaching newcomers what it means to belong to the organization. They are the basic stories of identity—and what is identity if not values, beliefs, behaviors, and aims?—that Gardner singles out as so important.

Hero Stories

Myths and hero stories readily fade into each other, but hero stories are much more common and sometimes lack the range and resonance of myths. Hero stories recount successes, most often triumphs achieved thanks to the courage and persistence of one individual. These are incentive stories that can inspire the listener to do likewise. The details of the story tell a lot about the culture. In some organizations, the typical hero story tells the tale of heroic gamble—a hero who risks everything for something he believes in, and wins. David Packard recounts one such story in *The HP Way*:

> *Chuck House was advised to abandon a display monitor he was developing. Instead, he embarked on a vacation to California—stopping along the way to show potential customers a prototype model of the monitor. . . . Their positive reaction spurred him to continue with the project even though, on his return to Colorado, he found that I, among others, had requested it be discontinued. He persuaded his R&D manager to rush the monitor into product, and as it turned out, HP sold more than seventeen thousand display monitors representing sales revenue of $35 million for the company.*

Ultimately, the story goes on, Packard honored House for "extraordinary contempt and defiance beyond the normal call of engineering duty."[24]

The main lessons of this story are clear: that the boss cares more about the success of the company than obedience, that he is willing to be proved wrong. Because it is vividly circumstantial and real, telling and retelling this story in the company is more likely to spur profitable disobedience than mission statement claims about meritocracy and risk taking. The story may not connect to the founding myths of HP as Art Fry's story does to the founding of 3M, but it is rich in other company values: the dedication that led House to show a product to customers during his so-called vacation, the value of getting independent confirmation, in this case from potential customers, of a personal hunch (of being, you might say, a sensible maverick). The story also illustrates the importance of persuasiveness and teamwork: House convinced his manager to engage in civil disobedience for the sake of the company. At team-oriented Hewlett-Packard, even the rebels work in teams.

People at UPS tell and retell stories of cooperation and devotion to getting the job done. As we mentioned in chapter 1, one story concerns an eight-months-pregnant center manager who delivered sixty packages in subzero weather when one of her drivers didn't show up. Drivers tell about making deliveries on schedule in weather that kept their competitors from FedEx off the roads. Those stories have the shape of many traditional heroic tales: the lone hero bravely facing a hostile world while lesser mortals fall by the wayside. From one perspective, comparing package deliveries to the quest for the Golden Fleece or the Holy Grail seems laughably extravagant. On the other hand, a modest but genuine echo of those heroic models contributes to driver fellowship and pride in the work.

FAILURE STORIES

Some failure stories are cautionary tales. They recount disastrous mistakes and what they mainly say is, Never, ever do this! The story of Xerox's failure to capitalize on its invention of the graphic user interface computer and the laser printer has become an icon for the company, fueling decades of effort to avoid a similar error in the future. Many failure stories illustrate offenses against the culture. There is the story circulating in one company, for instance, of the employee who overestimated the openness of the president's open-door policy and dropped in to shoot the breeze once too often. The story of his last days at the company helps others calibrate just how open that door is meant to be. Both "thou shalt nots" and "thou shalts" define cultures for their members.

Because most of us find failure stories particularly fascinating and persuasive, they travel freely by word of mouth. They are notoriously hard to capture in text or on videotape. People's reluctance to contribute the stories of their mistakes to "knowledge bases" often frustrates knowledge managers, because these stories often communicate more valuable learning than success stories do. British Petroleum has tried to circumvent the difficulty of capturing stories of failures by putting them in a positive form. For instance, rather than describe the problems that followed when one manager neglected to order critical materials on time, they constructed a hero story to emphasize the importance of timely ordering.[25] This is probably better than ignoring the issue altogether, but it drains away most of the power of stories: of particular circumstances and a particular voice, as well as the magnetic power of disaster—the same force that draws people to slow down to look at a wreck on the highway.

WAR STORIES

Within the safety of small groups and communities, failure stories are much easier to tell. People tell their coworkers about mistakes that they would not admit more publicly. Julian Orr recounts this story, the experience of someone relatively new to Xerox copier repair:

> *Until you break something good you're not a member of the team. . . . it did not occur to me to check the terminals, right, and that of course is something I'll never do again. You should have seen it: I had my back to the machine and smoke is rolling out of the card cage. And the lady says, "OHHH, I think we have a fire." And I say, "Oh, no problem," and went over and unplug it and say, "OK. Now I am a member of the team."*[26]

Sharing the story of a disaster directly with others can actually be a connecting experience, a builder of social capital—it helps make you a member of the team. Listeners who understand your work because they do it too are likely to grant a kind of forgiveness for the mistake: they often respond by describing the time the same or worse happened to them ("You think that's bad? Listen to what I once did.") They laugh, but their laughter comes from recognition, the sympathy of shared experience rather than the mockery of superiority and disapproval. So the story the Xerox tech rep tells on himself is a story of initiation, a kind of trial by fire (literally, in this case) that a challenging job inflicts on the people who take it on. The experience he describes marks the transition from being a novice who may still believe that manuals and training programs have all the answers, to a wiser, battle-scarred professional who knows how treacherous the real world can be.

In fact, the initiation story is a popular genre throughout our culture, frequently appearing as the plot or a subplot of film and TV dramas. We have all seen stories of the intern, rookie cop, raw recruit, or new kid on the block who learns the hard way that he still has a lot to learn. *How* he reacts to failure is more important than the inevitable fact of failure. The rookie who stubbornly continues to insist on doing it "by the book" is ostracized or fired, but the group of veterans welcomes the one made older and wiser by experience as one of them. Those TV plots are like little case studies in social capital that show how new people become (or fail to become) members of communities of practice.

The tech rep's story of surviving copier repair disaster creates a bond, a milder civilian version of the bond between soldiers in combat. And his story is about his response to disaster as much as about his error. When smoke poured out of the machine, he did not run screaming from the building or loudly curse Xerox for manufacturing a dangerous piece of junk. The fact that the rep's inexperience created the crisis does not negate the fact—is less important than the fact—that he proved himself by responding well to it. So failure stories can also be hero stories, stories of survival and membership: "This happened; it was horrible, but I got through it; I'm still here, and I'm one of you now—I understand what you deal with."

STORIES OF THE FUTURE

We have talked about the shared aims that characterize (and are a benefit of) organizations with high social capital. Members of cultures and companies can be united by a persuasive story of the future, a goal toward which they strive together. Some of the great political and social leaders of this century—Gandhi, Churchill, Martin Luther King, Jr.[27]—used stories of the future—of peaceful political independence, victory, racial justice—to create social capital, to draw people in to a cooperative effort, to make them a community. In his famous "I have a dream" speech, King talked about aspects of the equitable culture that "one day" will exist in the United States, repeatedly emphasizing the positive goals of the future over the problems of the present. His speech really meant, "We have a dream."

Few if any organizations have opportunities to operate at this level, but their stories of the future can also draw people together and even inspire them. We have already mentioned 3M's commitment to strategic plans in narrative form, because they are more vivid and persuasive than bullet-point plans and help people understand the actions and relationships needed to achieve the hoped-for future, as well as the desirability of achieving it.

Scenario planning is a version of storytelling about the future. In his discussion of scenarios, which he describes as "the memory of the future," Arie de Geus emphasizes the importance of good storytelling to useful and persuasive scenarios: "The person who writes the final draft . . . must be a good storyteller, with a nose for the main themes to be developed. The best-remembered scenarios, in fact, have some of the characteristics of fairy or folk tales."[28]

Consultant and cultural anthropologist Alanson Van Fleet notes the power stories have both to transmit the culture of the past and prepare for the future. "For centuries stories have served the dual purpose of holding societies and organizations together and creating portals for change," he says.[29] He describes using storytelling to help a manufacturer of technology for the textile industry and a healthcare organization to develop visions of the future that are persuasive, uniting, and inspiring.

Stories create a sense of membership and spur collaborative effort by telling those in the organizations who and what they collectively have been and are now, but also, and perhaps even more powerfully, stories draw people together by telling them what they can be in the future—*why* they are working together.

The Storytelling Occasion

Some twenty-five centuries ago, the citizens of Athens assembled at the theater of Dionysus every April. Somewhere between 10,000 and 20,000 of them attended the weeklong festival where, from dawn till dusk, they watched plays based on the myths they all knew—most dating back hundreds of years to Homer and before. The City Dionysia was an annual civic event, virtually compulsory for Athenian citizens. Both the plays themselves and the experience of watching them as a group fostered community. The retellings of familiar stories by Aeschylus, Sophocles, and others helped define what it meant—morally, socially, and politically—to be an Athenian and a human being. Commentaries on the culture's central myths, they simultaneously reflected and shaped how the Athenians saw themselves.

Place mattered to the dramatic storytelling that occurred in ancient Athens every April. It mattered, first of all, that the citizens gathered in one place so that the sharing of the dramas was a communal affair. Even the curved ranks of seating in the amphitheater contributed to a communal sense, allowing audience members to watch one another watching the drama and to see themselves situated in the community. The fact that performances occurred in daylight, not in a darkened hall, increased the sense of presence and participation. (The communal aspect of people these many centuries later watching the same television program in their separate homes and talking about it the next day is real, but weaker.) The location of the theater on the slopes of the Acropolis was partly a practical matter—the slopes created a natural amphitheater shape; freestanding amphitheaters came later—but it also brought it into proximity with the religious, commercial, and political center of Athens. As we have said, the location of social spaces matters. Their position at the heart or at the fringe of a city or organization reflects their importance, whether they are central or peripheral to its culture.

Stories read or heard on a recording can have power—we grudgingly admit the value of captured stories below. But stories told "live" in a social setting, even one less impressive than the Theater of Dionysus, have the added power of being social occasions and collaborative endeavors. Storytelling is collaborative in at least two senses. For one thing, storytelling means story listening, and listening to a story is an active process. The hearer of an effective story interprets and reconstructs it in terms of her own experience, "becomes" the hero of the story in some sense, compares what that hero does to what she might do and perhaps recasts the story in terms of similar situations she knows. The other element of collaboration has to do with reactive telling. A good storyteller (like a good stage actor) does not perform the same story precisely the same way every time he tells it. Even when the words are essentially the same, he adjusts pace, emphasis, pauses, and expression to his audience, responding to its response, even to the particular quality of silence the listening audience exhibits (experienced actors know that many detectably different kinds of silence exist). The mutual attentiveness of teller and listeners makes the storytelling a collaboration, a communication *between* rather than a broadcast *to*. This is one reason that stories on video are less effective than stories told face-to-face; recorded and played back, the story ceases to be collaborative and communal in quite the same powerful way.

John Pastore, formerly the chief technical officer of CapitalOne, believes people in organizations need to gather around a "virtual campfire" to tell each other stories in organizations. He remembers when his organization had only 700 associates and top decision-makers spent several hours a week in the same small meeting room, talking about the company and sharing their stories. Now that the company has grown to more than 12,000, creating an atmosphere conducive to storytelling is more challenging, as is the question of how to build a setting where storytelling is natural and expected. The assimilation program Pastore set up for new employees features experienced managers telling stories in a comfortable room. Molly Catron, who uses storytelling extensively in her work as organizational learning consultant at Eastman Chemical, favors storytelling rooms with no central table and people gathered in a circle.[30]

Even as new an organization as Viant has "folklore days" when veterans help newcomers understand what the company is all about by recounting their experiences from the "old days." The stories are important, but gathering to tell them may matter more. The World Bank's Steve Denning believes that the power of stories comes through speaking them to an audience and asserts that the act of storytelling is more important than the stories that are told.

CAPTURED STORIES

The dynamic nature of storytelling suggests that organizations should not blithely rush to capture stories in databases, on CD-ROMs, and videotapes—certainly not as a substitute for less-efficient but more powerful storytelling occasions. The advantages of captured stories are certainly clear. They can reach more people in more places; they are permanent assets rather than fleeting experiences. But even those advantages are drawbacks in disguise. Captured stories are distanced and secondhand, removed from the collaborative experience of the storytelling occasion. If you have ever seen a videotape of a stage play, you have experienced the tendency of that medium to flatten and dull a live event. Also, permanent means fixed; the teller of a captured story cannot connect with his audience by responding to their response. As Robert Sutton reminds us, captured stories are often "sanitized"—edited to match the self-image the organization wants to present. That means that some of the gritty, energetic, human details of real life may be edited out. The valuable unspeakable practices and revealing failures that people may be willing to share with a group of colleagues are unlikely to find their way onto a videotape or CD-ROM. Remember too that uncaptured stories have amazing staying power, as listeners become tellers and pass them along. Though not permanent or universally available, they persist and spread—sometimes for centuries or millennia. And each telling is a social interaction, tellers and listeners sharing an experience together.

Even with all of these qualifications (obviously we are not fans of canned stories), we admit that capturing the stories of retiring employees on video is better than letting the stories disappear with the people. When Diamond Technology Partners began to grow so quickly that newcomers were no longer certain to hear firm-origination stories firsthand, the company hired artificial intelligence pioneer Roger Schank to help them capture and distribute these tales of corporate identity. Schank had the founders of the firm record stories of its origin on videotape. New recruits could look at the video or a CD-ROM and learn why the firm was founded, what vision drove the effort, why it was named "Diamond." These informal stories connected them with the tradition and values of the organization. Leaders at Diamond Technology believe that the captured stories have helped transmit the culture. The important interactivity of the storytelling occasion is lost on video, but the medium at least has the advantage of relaying communication tone and body language along with words.

Some organizations collect their stories in archives and printed histories. Too often, though, this material is buried in back rooms of corporate libraries or unread books. There are ways to keep this material alive. At Procter & Gamble's corporate headquarters in Cincinnati, a museum-style display illustrating the company's history occupies a prominent place in the main lobby. Visitors are obviously a target audience, but the material is there for employees too, reminding them that they belong to a company with a long history of success based on products that have become part of the fabric of people's daily lives. Companies that employ archivists can consider making them not just custodians and organizers of historical materials, but corporate storytellers, carriers of the events that shape corporate identity who can explain the organization to itself in print and in person. In the Middle Ages, minstrels reflected the culture to itself and carried news and social knowledge from place to place. Perhaps the time has come to revive the tradition inside organizations.

Drama: Social Stories Enacted

The employees of a New England human resources firm sit in rows of chairs facing an improvised stage area at one end of their office, where two actor/consultants impersonate sales reps at a trade show. Working for an imaginary company called Hypergistics, they repeat canned sales pitches to a succession of invisible prospects. Despite these grating, rapid-fire spiels, they manage to snag one new client. A short play of four or five humorous scenes dramatizes the decline and fall of that new client relationship. It is first undermined by an obstructionist bureaucrat who says, "We can't get anything started until all the forms are in place." In the next scene, several company representatives promise to solve problems they don't understand and make no effort to coordinate their efforts. In the last scene, the frustrated client quits and Hypergistics employees are left wondering what went wrong. The actors are Gerard Donnellan and Nancy Carlson, of Big Leap Performance Solutions, a small Boston-area consulting firm that uses drama to reflect organizational culture back to a firm's members.

The "audience" responds with laughter and groans of recognition. At the end of the performance, Donnellan and Carlson invite employees to replay the scenes and fix the problems they saw enacted. Some are eager to participate. Others hesitate, but soon warm to the task. One reluctant performer eventually agrees to be a sales rep: "I have some ideas about how to find out what the client really wants, not just doing my little speech." Discussion of the company's real-life problems follows this revised performance. One person comments on the need to reduce and consolidate the paperwork they push on clients. Another sums it up: "We should concentrate on trying to make clients happy, not just making sure to do our own little jobs right."

Drama is hard to do well. Natural storytellers are more common than natural dramatists (or drama facilitators) in the world and the workplace. Many of the stories people tell feel authentic; drama—especially drama designed to make a point—frequently feels contrived. Used well, though, drama shares and even extends the ability of narrative to communicate emotion. Also, drama is preeminently social. Almost by definition, it is more about interactions between people than stories are. Stories usually focus on individuals in a social context—the success or failure of the hero facing whatever challenge the story describes. Drama comes into being when people relate to one another. The Big Leap performance described here showed a range of relationships in action that would be difficult to encompass in a story, and illustrated social capital themes of trust, understanding, communication, and collaboration. Stories probably do a better job of inspiring individuals to emulate the behavior of organizational heroes; drama puts individual behaviors more firmly in a social context.

With similar goals of engagement and capturing the social texture of the organization, Hewlett-Packard has used "Reader's Theatre" to make issues vivid and real. For instance (as Dorothy Leonard and Walter Swap recount), performing a script built from the actual experiences of gay and lesbian employees brought their experience to life for others in the company and influenced management's decision on benefits for same-sex partners.[31] Here too, theater works to illuminate the intersection of individual behavior and social milieu.

John M. Neill, chief executive of Unipart, the British auto parts firm, took on the task of transforming a corporate culture: of bridging a huge chasm between management and labor, moving from a confrontational organization to a participatory one. Among the many techniques he used to win over a skeptical, suspicious workforce was a three-hour theatrical event with musical numbers designed to convince members of the organization of the benefits of employee stock ownership. Both the emotional power of theater and its ability to unify an audience helped accomplish Neill's purpose. Given the difficulties of doing theater well and the coordination of resources needed to create it, drama will undoubtedly remain much less common in corporations than storytelling, but its particular social power can make it the right approach to some important, difficult situations.

Investments in Storytelling

As we have mentioned, storytelling is an essential leadership skill. In addition to communicating the values and norms of organizational culture, stories inspire action in ways that abstractions do not. Percy Barnevik, who helped shape industrial giant ABB as a decentralized federation of business units, spends most of his time traveling from unit to unit, telling stories about the firm and about what is happening in the other units. His job is not so entirely different from that of the minstrels and storytellers who knit past cultures together by carrying news, songs, and stories from place to place.

Training leaders in storytelling skills is one way to go, but probably has more drawbacks than advantages. Since authenticity and naturalness are part of what makes a good story, sending managers to storytelling school and then unleashing them and their newly learned, undigested techniques on the organization may actually be counterproductive. Simply getting people to tell stories is likely to be much more useful. Leaders can both validate the idea of storytelling and encourage others to tell stories by telling them themselves. Stories evoke stories. Most of us have been in meetings when someone—often a senior person—interrupts a dull flow of abstractions with a story. Immediately, someone else responds with another story, which reminds a third person of something similar (or opposite) that happened to her. Energy and engagement rise; people are suddenly communicating with one another about the real world of their work through stories. The most important investment in storytelling is the act of telling one.

In fact, some of the good news about stories is that they require so little investment of money or formal training. People in organizations mainly need some time and space for stories and permission to tell them—permission through example and through demonstrated respect for the value of stories. Specially designed storytelling settings—virtual campfires—can be helpful but are not necessary. Because storytelling is so natural to human beings, organizations need to do little more than give people a chance to tell them.

Giving them that chance—fostering a conversational, story-friendly environment—makes an essential contribution to social capital. The fact that no massive effort is required should not disguise the importance of making the investment. Storytelling and story listening build trust, understanding, and community. Real conversation and stories—social talk—are the heart of social capital. More than anything else, they bring people together and hold them together. It is no accident that *communicate* and *community* share the same Latin root.

Our next two chapters look at the important challenges of volatility and virtuality—which can themselves undermine organizational social capital but whose negative effects on organizations can be countered or moderated by high social capital. We present a number of ways of using social capital to manage volatility and virtuality, but none is more powerful than the social talk we have discussed here.

6

❖

THE CHALLENGE OF VOLATILITY

Nothing endures but change.
—HERACLITUS

THE SOFTWARE INDUSTRY offers a striking example of volatility in organizations. Silicon Valley companies lure bright young software designers away from one another with the bait of higher salaries and juicier stock options. Today's hot new product may be hotter tomorrow, or forgotten. Some firms double or triple in size in months and are swallowed by one of the technology giants. Others run through their venture capital and disappear, their ex-employees snapped up by growing companies hungry for more talent. Fortunes are made and lost. Job hopping is expected and seen (with some justification) as part of the creative ferment of the region. A recent *New York Times* article pegged the typical annual turnover rate of Silicon Valley companies at well over 20 percent.[1]

But look at SAS Institute, the world's largest privately held software company. In the two decades of its existence, SAS has grown from a company offering a single statistical analysis tool to a developer of data warehouse and decision-support software used by almost 4 million people at more than 30,000 user sites. SAS software organizes seat-and-route data for major airlines, manages clinical trial data for pharmaceutical companies, and calculates the consumer price index; it helps marine biologists track dynamic changes in fish stocks and analyzes masses of transaction data for most of the Fortune 100 companies. SAS Institute's turnover rate is below 4 percent. Long-term jobs are the rule, not the exception. As Stanford University's Jeffrey Pfeffer notes in a *New York Times Magazine* article on the issue of loyalty in a virtual age, "the company says that people will have three or four careers during their working lives and it hopes all will be at SAS."[2]

Rob Cross, director of advanced technology, who has been with the company for almost twenty years, says, "Salary levels at SAS are good but not extravagant. Annual salary is not what draws people here." One of the things that does is satisfying, engaging work. SAS Institute spends around 30 percent of its budget on R&D, giving its software engineers ample resources to develop and improve products. Cross explains, "SAS encourages people to move around if they want to, but a lot of people have a long-term relationship with a single project—some have spent twenty years on the mainframe program. They have a chance to supplant their own work with better work. There's a lot of sense of code ownership."[3]

The firm also achieves its high level of employee commitment through a culture of trust and respect, generous benefits, and recognition of the importance of people's personal lives—a value embodied in day care and recreational facilities and reasonable working hours. Although some SAS employees work long hours to get projects done, many work a thirty-five-hour week and adjust work schedules to meet family needs without endangering their careers. The company's respect for workers is reflected, says Cross, in an emphasis on "judgment, not rules" and little emphasis on hierarchy. There are no more than three or four levels between anyone in the company and President James Goodnight. No division exists between office dwellers and cubicle dwellers—everyone has an office. During one period of expansion, when people had to double up, Goodnight moved out of his large office into a smaller one so that two employees could use the space until a new facility was finished.

The mutual long-term commitment of employees and company pays off for SAS. Pfeffer says that its low turnover rate saves the company about $70 million a year (presumably measured against industry averages). Its stable workforce also supports a 98 percent customer retention rate. No revolving-door company could hope to build the kind of solid, responsive customer relationships that that figure suggests. The engineers committed to continued development of the code they "own" helps SAS incorporate 85 percent of customer requests for features and improvements into its products. Says Goodnight, "If you treat employees as if they make a difference to the company, they will make a difference to the company." *Fortune* magazine ranked SAS number three in its 1997 list of the 100 best companies to work for in America, and SAS made the top 10 in *Business Week*'s 1997 listing of the best companies for work and family.[4]

While magazine articles and books go on about free agency, contract work, and the death of loyalty, SAS Institute and many other successful organizations consciously strive to foster employee commitment, loyalty, and longevity. They see the value not only of hiring but of retaining talented employees—the benefits of relationship and membership as well as experience and expertise. If a fifth or more of an organization leaves every year, how can the people in it come to know and trust one another, and how can the organization maintain its sense of what it is and how it does things? Thoughtful commentators including Arie de Geus, Frederick Reichheld, and Sumantra Ghoshal and Christopher Bartlett point to the continuing (and perhaps increasing) importance of loyalty, continuity, and longevity. Speaking at the 1998 Knowledge Forum at the Haas School at Berkeley, Peter Drucker said the following:

> *The challenge is to make the knowledge worker want to stay with the corporation, want to contribute and be productive. Turnover has always been expensive, but today your means of production can walk out the door. You need them more than they need you. They are not "assets"—assets can be bought and sold, yet they are the only value.*[5]

The forces driving volatility are real. Mobility, exciting opportunities, and (as we write) extremely low unemployment tempt people to move from job to job. Organizations change their composition and even their aims and behaviors in the face of global competition, converging companies and technologies, new products, and new customer demands. But rather than celebrate volatility or simply accept its consequences, some organizations work hard to limit it and counter its potentially destructive effects on social capital.

The fact that these are volatile times is part of our motivation for writing. "The challenge of volatility" refers both to the ways volatility challenges social capital and the ways that attention to social capital can help organizations deal successfully with volatility that might otherwise threaten their cohesion and the commitment and cooperative of their employees. Existing social capital and especially deliberate investment in social capital in times of stress and change can help organizations preserve their essential values, connections, and skills—their essential identities—in potentially disruptive situations.

We have alluded to two elements of volatility. One is the volatility of talent at a time when the battle to retain good workers is at least as important a part of the "war for talent" as the battle to attract outstanding people in the first place. The other is organizational volatility: the changing practices and policies, the mergers and acquisitions and hirings and firings that organizations undertake to master changing competitive environments. The two are connected, of course. Tactics in the battle to retain talent include taking steps to hold on to good people during periods of disruption and difficulty. But organizations trying to solve the problem of volatility must deal with two related but different questions:

- How do we bind new employees to the organization?

- How do we maintain trust relationships, networks, and shared aims and understandings in the organization in the face of potentially disruptive change?

The first question asks how organizations turn newcomers into committed members of the group; the second, how that sense of membership—and social capital in general—survives when some of the rules of the group change.

Building Commitment

We start with the first question and an example of a company trying to create a committed workforce in a young, volatile industry through its hiring practices and the process it uses to assimilate new people into the organization.

Viant is a small, growing company, barely five years old, that helps organizations design and build electronic businesses. Whether it continues to grow and prosper in the fluid world of Web-business consulting remains to be seen, but Viant, under the leadership of CEO Bob Gett, devotes significant time and resources to attracting and holding on to good workers in an industry in which job hopping is expected.[6] He believes that the number one crisis for growing businesses is "access to talent, and keeping that talent after you've invested two or three years in developing it." Gett believes that the long-term commitment of people who have genuinely become part of the organization, who have absorbed the "Viant DNA," gives the company a competitive advantage. This conviction supports both careful attention to hiring and assimilation processes and Gett's determination to grow the company "organically" rather than through acquisitions that dilute the company's sense of identity or set up clashes between cultures.

Hiring for the Long Term

Candidates for jobs at Viant are judged more in terms of cultural fit than experience or sheer intelligence. Bob Gett explains, "Our definition of 'best' is not the conventional one of people with the most experience or accomplishments in their careers. It is more about how they interact with each other in a team setting. What we're developing is less hard skills than a way of working." As a result, most hiring decisions are made only after a lengthy period of interviews with multiple people. As Gett remarks, "You've got to hang out with people for a while before you know them." As many as eight Viant employees who will work directly with the new hire interview candidates on the same day and then get together to discuss them. "When the group talks together and compares observations," Gett comments, "they begin to understand the candidate. And if the group says, 'OK, Harry is right for us,' then he starts with eight people believing in him. The interview process begins to make him part of a team."

In other words, the hiring process itself begins to create a network of connections that will help integrate the new person into the company. The newcomer starts with advocates and potential mentors; he is on the way to being part of the culture before he officially joins it.

Many organizations that strive for high social capital and long-term stability similarly hire for cultural fit. At Russell Reynolds Associates, at least ten people interview candidates for each recruiting position, and CEO Hobson Brown screens every hiring decision in the eighteen countries where the firm has offices to make sure candidates have the requisite "sociability and cooperative spirit." RRA's willingness to forgo clear economic gain in favor of cultural compatibility shows how seriously it takes the issue. The company recently considered hiring a very senior recruiter with outstanding skills, knowledge, and an undoubtedly valuable network of personal connections—the bread and butter of executive recruiting, some might argue. Negotiations broke down because he was clearly unwilling to be a team player; Russell Reynolds Associates would not compromise its belief in the centrality of peer relationships, despite the profit potential of his joining the firm, and chose not to offer him a job.

Some companies that value cultural fit, lasting relationships, and collaboration have invented ways of establishing working relationships with potential employees so that they can gather even more extensive evidence for judging fit. IDEO, the product design firm that relies on collaborative brainstorming to develop many of its new product ideas, gets to know job candidates very well. Some of the firm's senior staff at its Palo Alto home office teach in the master's program in engineering design in Stanford University's Mechanical Engineering Department. They essentially conduct a three-year "interview" of promising designers who are students in their classes and often also have internships at the company. At the end of that time, IDEO has a clear sense both of candidates' abilities and their compatibility with the company culture, and the successful candidates understand a great deal about IDEO.[7]

ORIENTATION AND TRAINING

It is hard to enthusiastically recommend orientation and training, since much of it is so badly done. Even the best programs struggle with the drawback of being removed from real work and real work environments. Employees often resent time away from their "real jobs" and see little practical value in what they are taught. Nevertheless, some orientation and training programs can be a useful part of the process of integrating and aligning new people, of moving them toward membership. (*Orient* literally means "turning to the east" and, by extension, getting one's bearings or turning in the right direction.)

Successful orientation programs put as much or more emphasis on communicating cultural behaviors and values as on teaching skills and procedures that probably do not match how work is really done. Because they strive to initiate newcomers into what the company is really like, they are best taught by active veterans than by full-time trainers or—worse—outside training specialists hired to introduce new employees to a company they only know at second hand. Their participation also means that newcomers and veterans get to know one another. In fact, connecting with people from other parts of the company may be the single best justification for orientation programs. For all these reasons, needless to say, the best orientation programs cannot be solely Web- or CD-ROM-based.

Bob Gett sees the mandatory three-week Viant training program as, in part, an opportunity to "scrape off some of the junk they got from prior organizational learning." The teachers of Viant's training are company veterans who bring their own experience of the work to the case studies and projects in the course. Viant's program is always taught at a single site, in Boston, so that people hired by the company's eight offices can begin to form personal networks that will help them in their work and help hold the company together. For three weeks, participants from all Viant offices spend most of the day together in intensive sessions, and they stay in the same apartment building at night. They return to their separate offices with contacts that span the company.

New hires at Russell Reynolds Associates now get an orientation module when they start their careers at the firm which contains much of the explicit information that used to be part of the new associates programs. Relieved of the necessity to teach that material, the program sessions they attend within their first six months focus on acculturation as well as bonding and relationship building. As at Viant, company veterans introduce newcomers to the company. Seasoned RRA partners teach the new associates sessions, so most of the work consists of cases, role-playing, and "war stories" told by the individuals who have lived them. Often these teacher/trainers are area or country managers, practice leaders, or out-standing search professionals from around the world who are flown in for the program. They give the content the stamp of real experience. Their participation also provides additional opportunities for new members to meet and form bonds with one another and with the leaders of the firm. At Russell Reynolds, these social/business connections are an explicit goal of the program, according to Alice Early, who directed the Russell Reynolds training program for almost a decade. She adds, "When the sessions are in New York, new associates attend a cocktail reception at the New York office where they meet the people they need to know to get things done and make things happen."[8] Early says too that participants in the Russell Reynolds program become a "class" whose members tend to stay connected, as members of college classes often do. They form cross-office, cross-practice, and cross-border relationships that they draw on during their subsequent careers with the firm.

Needless to say, these program are costly. They demand money and attention in industries under pressure to meet client needs quickly. They demonstrate commitment to transmitting organizational values and norms and to building strong connections between the firm and new employees and among the members of the firm. They provide a vivid example of social capital investment made in the expectation of long-term returns.

Longevity

The assimilation processes described above and the SAS Institute example with which we started this chapter suggest some of the things good companies do to retain talented employees. Close ties to others in the organization and identification with organizational values and aims are more reliable bases for longevity than the promise of a lot of money. When John Seely Brown says that organizations need to understand and tap identity formation, he recognizes that work is a primary source of an individual's self-esteem. Though money matters a great deal in this society, it is not everything, and organizational leaders should ask themselves if they want to hire people who only "follow the money." Explaining why his firm does not offer up-front bonuses to entice experienced brokers to join, Ben Edwards, CEO of A. G. Edwards, explains, "It would tend to attract the wrong kind of people and it would be unfair to our loyal employees. The message would be that the best way to make a lot of money is to jump around from firm to firm."[9] This suggests a further problem with trying to buy loyalty: mercenaries are "loyal" to the highest bidder, ready to move on when the inevitable better offer comes along or when the company's rosy future dims. Those who live by the stock option will die by the stock option. As we write, many dot-com companies that attracted employees with promises of stock-option wealth a year or two down the road are struggling to hold on to them now that the value of company stock has dropped.

LONGEVITY AND SOCIAL CAPITAL

Longevity builds social capital because relationships and trust develop over time. Other things being equal, the longer people stay in an organization, the more they will know and understand one another and the deeper and more extensive their networks of relationships will tend to be. London School of Economics professor Richard Sennett remarks, "The short time frame of modern institutions limits the ripening of informal trust. . . . Strong ties depend on long association. And more personally they depend on a willingness to make commitments to others."[10]

Some of the benefits of longevity are easily measurable—most obviously, reduced costs of hiring and training. A few years ago, an engineering group at Hewlett-Packard calculated that it took twenty-five months to get a new engineer up to speed, and $150,000 would be invested in that individual before the company began to see a return.[11] Greater trust and richer knowledge of the organization and people in it are also benefits. Long-term employees are often repositories of organizational stories who pass on important legends and emblematic tales to newcomers, ensuring continuity. We also suggest (with Frederick Reichheld) that longevity helps organizations build customer loyalty. Although not synonymous, longevity and loyalty are closely related: most people who stick with an organization are loyal to it and identify its interests with their own to a significant extent. Reichheld says, "Employees who are not loyal are unlikely to build an inventory of customers who are." He notes the time it takes to build solid relationships with customers and adds, "the same business philosophy and operational policies that earn employees' loyalty and boost their morale are likely to work for customers."[12]

Reflecting on what is now an almost fifteen-year partnership, managers at Boston Financial and New York Life Mainstay Funds attribute their successful relationship in part to the long-term involvement of key players from both companies. That stability has led to strong trust relationships—to mutual confidence that one partner company *does* understand the other's issues in all their complexity. Among other things, this confidence and trust have helped the partnership weather change and allowed Boston Financial to provide the innovative technologies that met real client needs. While pointing to specific innovations that have marked the collaboration between the two groups, longtime Boston Financial Senior Vice President Paul O'Neil sees maintaining a successful relationship through more than ten years of change as Boston Financial's most important accomplishment. Moving into its second decade, the relationship remains strong. "This is not a sprint." he says. "We're marathoners."[13]

Holding on to good employees reduces volatility—obviously, since high turnover forms part of our definition of volatility. Longevity also helps reduce the disruptive effects of unavoidable volatility. The people who know the company well, embody its values, and trust one another can help pilot it through the rough seas of new partnerships, competitive challenges, and initiatives.

MEASURING RETENTION RATES

Longevity is one social capital indicator and benefit that has the additional advantage of being fairly easy to measure. In fact, most organizations already track retention or turnover rates. Many organizations compare their rates with those of other firms in the same industry, assuming (as SAS Institute and HP do, for instance) that a turnover rate lower than the industry average indicates a relatively higher level of satisfaction and commitment, as well as less money spent on recruitment and training and greater continuity and cohesion. In some fields that have traditionally high turnover rates, though—some consulting firms, with annual turnover as high as 30 percent, come to mind—being at or slightly better than the average may not be cause for celebration or complacency. Revolving-door companies need to calculate the costs and benefits of high turnover. If the costs outweigh the benefits, they should examine the assumptions, structures, and culture behind the statistics regardless of how they stack up against the competition.

Statistics alone do not tell the whole retention story. Who leaves and why also matter. The first Ford Taurus was designed by a community of engineers brought together from various parts of the company. The project was a huge success, but within a few years every major contributor to it had left Ford—a loss that deserved but never received analysis. As Sumantra Ghoshal and Christopher Bartlett point out, many firms that strive for stability, commitment, and maximization of their human resources try to understand why good people leave:

> The best firms don't simply track defection rates; they categorize departures and then track defection rates by category. MBNA, for instance, tries very hard to be an excellent place to work, so when an employee who's performing well quits, the company does an exit interview to find out why. . . . People who leave because their spouses have been transferred to the west coast are not lumped in with people who are going down the street to work for a competitor.[14]

Weathering Change: Mending the Social Contract

We can think of the promises, expectations, and benefits that connect individuals and organizations as a social contract—a mainly tacit agreement about expected behaviors, agreed-upon values, and what the parties in the relationship agree to give and expect to get. Some of the terms of the agreement between an employee and a firm are quite explicit, of course. Written contracts specify the new employee's position, salary, and benefits, and may include clauses about ownership of intellectual property, confidentiality, and the like. But most of the agreement—the social contract that defines much of the relationship—is not spelled out in writing. It includes many of the expectations that make a job worthwhile and binds individuals to the organization: the promise of interesting work; expectations of recognition and advancement; a cooperative environment; respect; opportunities to make decisions and initiate projects and so forth.

As Professor Denise Rousseau points out in *Psychological Contracts in Organizations* and as earlier discussion in this chapter suggests, the terms of this implicit contract are negotiated over time, by many people in many situations. How recruiters and managers talk about the company and the position being offered is part of the negotiation, defining an often informal but powerful set of promises. Even the reputation of a company (or candidate) before they meet begins to "write" the contract. For instance, Hewlett-Packard has a (generally well-deserved) reputation for being a good place to work, with opportunities to work cooperatively on a variety of interesting projects. If a new hire at HP finds this not to be true, he may feel that an agreement has been broken, unless his conversations with the company have made it clear that his impression of its reputation is wrong. Equally important are what Rousseau calls "ongoing repetitive interactions," the behaviors during work that continually reinforce or redefine the terms of the relationship.[15]

In her research, Rousseau found that many of the people who were dissatisfied with their jobs felt that promises about their opportunities and the nature of their work implied in interviews and conversations during the "wooing" period had not been kept. What is true of courtships between individuals also goes for the courtship between a firm and a potential new member: A courtship that promises too much is likely to mean a disappointing and unhappy marriage.

The social and psychological contract between an employee and an organization is never entirely fixed. As Rousseau puts it, "Today's contract performance changes tomorrow's contract terms."[16] A wide range of events and circumstances—performance reviews, new responsibilities, conversations with supervisors, leaders' statements about the aims and values of the business, to name a few—redefine or renegotiate it to one degree or another. It defines a living relationship, which means a changing one. But this expected adjustment occurs in the context of core expectations that remain the same. Changing those central provisions breaks the contract and threatens to destroy the relationship (and social capital with it). Trust, cooperation, and a sense of equity are all at stake. Threats to core beliefs, behaviors, and expectations threaten the sense of membership in general: witness the religious and political groups split by differences that one faction sees as a betrayal of a group's identity.

The most familiar business example of contract breaking is the downsizing that occurs in organizations with a tradition (and implied promise) of long-term employment for workers who remain productive and fulfill "their side of the bargain." Though few companies explicitly guarantee lifetime jobs in return for commitment and hard work, the widespread sense of betrayal that downsizing caused shows how powerful the expectation of job security in exchange for skill and commitment has been. Social contracts are broken locally too. These breaches are less publicly visible than are large-scale events like downsizing, but they happen every day and the damage they do, though less dramatic, may ultimately be greater. They happen, for instance, when a supervisor denies an employee decision-making opportunities that she has been led to expect, or when promised opportunities to learn new skills are lost so that employees can keep up with daily work demands.

How can organizations help maintain their social contracts with members and limit damage when breaking them is unavoidable, when economic conditions or the volatility of an industry make changes necessary that threaten the contract's terms?

First, they need to be aware of what those terms are, and recognize that implied expectations are often more powerful than explicit contract clauses. As Denise Rousseau points out, tradition, observed behaviors, and the expectations of peers all contribute to the social contract. An employer who is unaware of the implicit terms of the bargain with employees may be blindsided by the betrayal they express when one of these hidden provisions is violated. A legalistic focus on the written contracts ("Where is the clause that says you would spend half your time on research?") misses the point that the dispute is about the nature of a relationship and the terms of membership, not the details of impersonal transactions that most formal contracts define. And an employer who sticks to the letter of the law regarding what it owes employees—who reduces a relationship to transactions—will have employees who obey the letter of the law when it comes to what they owe the company. Experience shows that "working to rule" can bring most organizations to their knees.

But not every major change is a breach of contract. Rousseau says, "Substitution is actually a common form of contract keeping." She adds that "a breach of contract occurs when one party reneges on the agreement *despite their ability to fulfill it*"[17] (italics ours). If management persuasively demonstrates that change—even as drastic a change as downsizing—is necessary for the health and survival of the firm, then perceptions of betrayal and bad faith on the part of the organization are reduced or avoided. And if the painful process is carried out and seen to be carried out fairly, that too makes a positive difference. So leaders of organizations should make the reasons for changes in the contract clear and demonstrate that the necessary pain is being shared as equitably as possible. Leaders who lay off workers to cut costs while granting themselves larger and larger bonuses breed resentment and cynicism.

The action taken by Hewlett-Packard when its business temporarily declined in the seventies was very different. David Packard says,

> Because of a downturn in the U.S. economy . . . [w]e were faced with the prospect of a 10 percent layoff. Rather than a layoff, however, we . . . went to a schedule of working nine days out of every two weeks—a 10 percent cut in work schedule with a corresponding 10 percent cut in pay. . . . The net result of this program was that effectively all shared the burden of the recession, good people were not released into a very tough job market, and we had our highly qualified workforce in place when business improved.[18]

This approach turned a situation that could have diminished social capital into a social capital builder. It said, as clearly as possible, "we're all in this together." Both at that time and for many years later (as a powerful story of equity and solidarity), it built trust and a sense of membership in a collaborative enterprise. As we mentioned early on, change—even difficult change—accomplished *with* rather than *against* the members of the organization can actually increase social capital, fostering a sense of solidarity in crisis.

Part of a persuasive argument for serious change is recognition of its cost, including its emotional cost. One of the authors witnessed an oil company CEO openly upset when lower oil prices compelled him to announce layoffs at his organization. His expressions of feeling did not change the facts or put food in the mouths of the people who lost their jobs, but they made a big difference to the people who left and those who stayed. Various commentators have noted that downsizing makes the "survivors" feel less secure. Because of the CEO's behavior in this case, employees felt safe from job cuts driven by pure greed or arbitrary displays of power. Their leader's genuine concern about their fate convinced them that the cuts were critical to the company's success and would not be repeated unless a similarly difficult situation arose.

Sometimes too organizations need to admit that a change that makes sense on paper exacts too high a social cost, and change their minds. For instance, in 1999 IBM modified its pension policy. This seemed to make economic and organizational sense for the company, but some longtime employees who stuck with IBM during its lean years in the late eighties and early nineties felt that the rules were being changed to their detriment in the middle of the game. The betrayal this "broken promise" caused them to feel was too high a price for the company to pay for the apparent advantages of the new plan. In response, IBM rescinded the change for a significant percentage of the affected employees.

Managing Change at UPS

The social contracts at United Parcel Service have long included the expectation of promotion from within. Coming up through the ranks has had something like the force of a religious tenet or defining principle. The UPS "story" has always been one of people moving gradually through the company and of leaders who understand from personal experience what it means to be a driver or package sorter. The UPS values of hard work, versatility, broad understanding, and competence (rather than specialized brilliance) support the principle. Commitment, a cardinal value, is consonant with promotion from within, as is the UPS idea of success as a gradual accumulation of reputation, responsibility, and financial reward.

Jeff Sonnenfeld and Meredith Lazo's Harvard Business School case documents the emotional and practical difficulties of UPS's decision to modify this policy. In the eighties, the need for staff with high-level information technology skills was indisputable, but company leaders feared the damage that compromising the old ideal might do to the company's culture and, especially, to the powerful implied contract with employees. Sonnenfeld observes that some employees,

> after hearing in their interviews and reading in the Policy Book that promotion-from-within was one of the most honored UPS policies, were confused and disappointed when they saw outside hires being placed in positions they thought they were being trained for. Some felt they had been misled. One entry-level programmer commented, "It's frustrating that management is not following the promotion-from-within policy. I understand that people with greater expertise are needed, but I wish they would have told us the real policy during orientation."[19]

In part, the organization managed this difficult change of policy by making the need for it clear. As Denise Rousseau suggested, changes that are understood to be necessary for the continued success or survival of the organization are not seen as breaches of contract, as more capricious changes are.

UPS has also taken seriously the cultural issue of making sure that the newcomers adapt to the culture rather than transform it to a less desirable one. Even in skill areas like information technology, which would seem to have little in common with package delivery, the company consciously strives to hire the kind of people who will fit the traditional culture. UPS also uses orientation programs to acclimatize newcomers to the culture. In addition to attending training and orientation programs, many managerial new hires spend time at a sorting center or on a package car route to get a feel for the traditional UPS experience. (McKinsey, too, makes new employees at every level work on diverse projects before assuming much responsibility.) Ken Parks of human resources comments on the orientation process:

> How do you infuse the culture into experienced folk who come in at a high level? It takes time for them to embrace it. After a few months, they start to

say the same things as UPSers. They say "we," not "I" (except when taking responsibility for a mistake). The IS group includes a lot of people hired quickly. We made sure to include a lot of UPSers in the group. They didn't have the same level of technical skills as the new hires, but they had cultural skill.[20]

To an outsider, the persistence of long-standing organizational norms at UPS seems more remarkable than the slippage. Promotion from within is still a company-defining expectation—no longer universal but still the desirable norm. The effects of change are unpredictable, though. Over time, the modification of the promotion-from-within policy may prove more of a problem than it currently appears to be. The more recent decision to sell shares of UPS stock to the public for the first time is another change that makes business sense but whose long-term effects on the culture are unknown. (Recognizing the importance of private ownership, the company has made only 10 percent of its stock and 1 percent of voting rights available to the public.)

Some change, of course, invigorates organizations and can help avoid the clannishness of "the ties that blind." Ideally, UPS could get the best of both worlds: new skills, new flexibility, and new ideas, invigorating traditional values, norms, and behaviors. Dan McMackin, a twenty plus year UPS veteran and public relations manager, notes that outsiders help "keep the company from being inbred. There is value in having different viewpoints; we need people with vision, not just good drivers."[21] The ideal is seldom achieved, though, and it is hard to imagine UPS getting all the benefits of new blood with no dilution of the "brown blood" that has kept the company going for almost a hundred years. New viewpoints probably take a toll on old cohesion. McMackin recognizes the danger: "As we get bigger, there's a dance to be done between being inbred and losing our identity."

A similar dance goes on in many high-social-capital companies that must change to keep pace with a changing world while trying to hold on to their best traditional elements, their sources of trust, purpose, and committed membership. We believe that organizational awareness of the importance of membership and willingness to value the implicit contracts that support it can help them perform this difficult balancing act. In some unavoidable circumstances of crisis or challenge, organizations are forced to draw on their social capital. Sometimes companies respond to the crisis of lower sales or stock market valuation by cutting back on the very things—from orientation to more open opportunities to travel budgets for internal meetings—that build social capital. Instead, they should recognize the threat these situations pose to trust and collaboration and devote resources and attention to repairing damaged connections and replenishing potential social capital losses.

Employee Surveys

Ongoing surveys of employee satisfaction can help guide social capital investments at any time, but especially during periods of volatility. They are one of the tools organizations can use both to measure trends in social capital and identify particular problems. Both Motorola and Hewlett-Packard use regular employee surveys to find and fix local problems. Motorola's Individual Dignity Entitlement program treats any negative response to questions about the meaningfulness of work or managerial support as quality failures that must be addressed.[22] The fact of a survey—especially one supported by a long-term commitment of attention and resources—also demonstrates that management recognizes the value of the social health of the organization.

According to Paul Siemion of UPS's human resources department, the company's commitment to a universal annual employee survey grew out of basic social capital questions that company leaders raised at the 1992 annual management conference.[23] They asked, "How do we improve employee relations? How do we capitalize on the spirit of the organization?" In other words, how could the company increase its social capital and get more value from it? Part of the response was an employee relations index (ERI) survey that would give every center manager an annual report on working relationships with his or her people, and give every employee an opportunity to make his or her concerns known. Company leaders believed the survey could identify local problems that managers would immediately address, but they also recognized that it could also be used to diagnose trends in the "spirit" or social health of the organization. In practice, it has helped UPS gauge the impact of potential divisive situations (like the 1997 Teamsters strike) and of efforts to repair damage they might cause.

The ERI survey includes questions about the fairness of opportunities for advancement, the cooperativeness of coworkers, openness and trust in the working environment, the degree to which good work is recognized, and the accessibility of managers and their openness to new ideas. It also asks participants how confident they are that management will act on problems identified by the survey. Though far from a complete analysis of organizational social capital, it gives managers and the company as a whole important indications of trends in trust, communication, cooperation, and perceived equity—all important social capital factors.

To make sure that the ERI survey is more than "just a piece of paper," the company invests in an infrastructure to administer it and (especially) to oversee responsive action. Each of UPS's sixty districts has a full-time employee relations (ER) manager; others work at the regional and corporate level, for a total of about seventy-five employees directly responsible for making the survey work. (Most ER managers also have related responsibilities, including training and resolving disputes that involve nonunion employees.) ER managers promote and administer the survey, ensure confidentiality, bring results to the centers, and make sure that a follow-up meeting takes place. In characteristic UPS fashion, results are dealt with locally in face-to-face meetings of employees with their immediate supervisors. ER managers also help centers develop action plans to make necessary improvements. Participation rates have usually been above 75 percent and as high as 81 percent. Immediately after the Teamsters strike, participation fell to 72 percent, but it climbed again past 76 percent in the fall of 1998.

In many organizations, employee survey analysis takes so long that it reflects what the organization was like last year and therefore loses much of its value. At UPS, ERI survey results are returned quickly so they will be relevant to the current situation, and to make sure that problems are promptly addressed. District staff get results three days after the surveys are completed; centers see results in a week. Even the overall corporate report that aggregates local results is generated within two weeks of the survey date. The company's investment in staff to manage the survey and response process, its determination to respond rapidly, and the importance it attaches to the overall results demonstrate and communicate its conviction that social capital, in the form of these relationships, is important.

ER managers use the survey to identify "most help needed" centers and devote a lot of their attention to changing behaviors there. At a corporate level, the survey provides analysis that can lead to future action. Tracing the rise and fall of the overall index gives the company a measure of how it's doing. Corporate analysts are also beginning to relate employee satisfaction measures to other important indicators and results such as injury statistics, retention rates for part-time employees, and safety statistics. They are considering exploring other correlations—for instance, between customer satisfaction and favorable ERI responses from package car drivers. Survey results are part of UPS's balanced scorecard measure, which looks at organizational performance from four perspectives: people, customers, financial, and operational. Though far from an exact measure of social capital, the ERI survey gives a clear relative calibration of the levels of trust, communication, and connection in the company. The increasingly sophisticated analysis of its results promises to provide important indications of the economic value of these social goods.

Lucent Technologies Value in People survey similarly looks at the state of the organization's culture from the employee's point of view. According to Sue Klepac, Inventor of Possibilities at Lucent, 78 percent of employees respond to the survey, a figure that itself suggests confidence in the organization's commitment to cultural issues.[24] Hewlett-Packard's semiannual employee survey also addresses social capital issues. Like the Motorola Individual Dignity Entitlement survey, it is designed to identify and quickly redress people's problems. Neither company, though, aggregates local results to generate the kind of overall evaluation that UPS has developed and continues to expand. The localness of these social capital assessments makes some sense. Just as "all politics is local," so all social capital is local (virtually by definition; since it consists of relationships, it can only exist between people, not as some quality "out there"). Though global actions affect local social capital for good or ill, local interventions are also important. We believe, however, that not aggregating local results into a general evaluation is a lost opportunity. At any time, these surveys can be an important tool for measuring social capital. In times of change, they can provide valuable information about how best to repair social capital damage.

Investments in Stability

We believe that the disruptions, uncertainties, and even the expanded possibilities of a volatile age make social capital more important than ever. With the boundaries of organizations remade again and again by mergers, acquisitions, and shifting partnerships, with global teams forming and disbanding and firms continually looking for new ideas, established trust relationships, mutual understanding, commitment, and other elements that characterize high social capital provide the stability and connection that allow organizations to hold together and members of organizations to work together. We all use our established personal networks and communities as tools for making sense of the world, and sense making is one of the most difficult and important activities people and organizations undertake in a changing and uncertain world.

Because volatility threatens social capital and because existing social capital helps manage volatility successfully, leaders need to be aware of the social capital effects of the changes affecting their organizations and take steps to preserve and rebuild their social capital stocks. Social capital surveys can be one item on that agenda. More important, we think, is continued appreciation for social capital and varied investment in it at a time when many cutting-edge commentators argue that some of its essential elements are dead, dying, or outmoded.

One factor affecting organizational volatility that we have not emphasized in this chapter is virtuality: both the idea of the virtual corporation and the communications technology behind telecommuting, virtual teaming, and other forms of work-at-a-distance. The possibility of working online and of people meeting electronically to carry out particular projects certainly contributes to the sense that jobs and organizations, no longer firmly anchored in particular places and times or limited to a local workforce, can change quickly. The subject of virtuality, so important in itself and so deeply connected with social capital issues, is discussed in chapter 7.

7

❖

THE CHALLENGE OF VIRTUALITY

The new means of communication accentuate
and strengthen non-communication.
—OCTAVIO PAZ

ONE OF THE AUTHORS was at Logan Airport about to board an early shuttle flight to New York when his cell-phone rang. It was his wife, relaying a message that the meeting in Manhattan had been canceled. Happy not to have to make the trip, he watched other businesspeople boarding the plane and began to wonder what was taking them to New York City so early in the morning. He decided to ask. He spent the next two hours or so in the boarding area, asking nearly fifty travelers where they were going and why.

About half of the people he informally surveyed were on their way to internal company meetings. They were using time and money and facing the typical annoyances of air travel and taxicab rides to spend, at most, two or three hours with colleagues. He asked if they had access to videoconferencing equipment. Nearly all said that they did, and of course everyone had e-mail, faxes, and telephones. When he asked why they did not use those technologies to participate in the meeting, their responses varied but touched on similar themes: "I need to be there in person or my budget will be cut"; "They will make some boneheaded decision if I'm not there"; "It wouldn't look good if I didn't show up"; and, most commonly, "I just *need* to be there."

These responses speak to the importance of social capital: the connections and conversations that maintain trust, relationship, reliability, and mutual understanding, the importance of commitment and membership. Organizations have intranets, e-mail, teleconferencing, and videoconferencing at their disposal, but the skies are full of planes bringing people together, attesting to both a deep human and organizational need and the limitations of virtuality. We believe that virtual work poses a challenge to social capital but is not always its enemy. Almost certainly, virtual work will have increasingly and varied roles in organizations in the future; here we look at virtuality from a social capital perspective.

Virtual Work

We think of virtual work as any work done over distance, with critical connections made by e-mail, intranets, videoconferencing, cellphones, and other new communications technology. Most of it is work that was traditionally done in the immediate vicinity of other workers located in the same office or laboratory: product development, research, developing plans and proposals, organizing and carrying out client engagements. Telecommuting "road warriors" checking their e-mail from hotel rooms and airplanes and global teams and dispersed communities of practice are now familiar examples of people engaged in virtual work. "Virtuality" also has to do with new thinking about organizations themselves, especially of the "virtual corporation" as a cluster or network of usually dispersed individuals who come together around a particular project or task and disband when they have completed it. This activity does not absolutely depend on the communications technology of virtuality. The most commonly cited examples of successful virtual organizations—the cast and crew who make a film, or freelance musicians who record a CD together—rely on gathering people at one spot much more than collaborating over distance. Nevertheless, proponents of virtual corporations generally and correctly see them depending on the technology of virtuality for coordination and collaboration. So these two ideas of virtuality are not the same, but they overlap and raise the same social capital issues.

The social capital implications of virtuality are complicated, but the questions at least are fairly clear. To what extent can people develop and maintain social capital by electronic means? Can the trust-building, network-building meetings and conversations we have described as sources of social capital occur virtually? Does virtual work increase or diminish social capital? Can we use our understandings of social capital to help make virtual work possible and to suggest ways to improve and supplement the technology of virtuality? We do not expect to answer these questions thoroughly, but we do want to come to grips with them.

Admitting Our Ignorance

We are writing about this subject in the middle of a worldwide social and organizational experiment whose results we cannot confidently predict. The Internet, e-mail, cellphones, and laptop computers are changing how we work and live, influencing home lives and vacations as well as workdays, testing and transforming our definitions of connection, community, the workplace, and leisure, and affecting our sense of the speed of life and the distinctions we make between global and local issues and between private and public life. The capacity that advances in computing give us to send information quickly and cheaply over distance has helped drive globalization, and globalization has increased the need to coordinate and collaborate over distance. The pursuit of efficiency, the desire to save time and money, and the belief that global companies need to bring their resources of knowledge, judgment, and creativity together regardless of distance have led to the creation of global teams and virtual communities, to the elevation of e-mail to a central place in the workday, and to the widespread use of teleconferencing and videoconferencing.

Organizations have been making these major changes with no direct knowledge of their long-term effects and often with surprisingly little explicit attention to how they will influence learning, creativity, coherence, and cohesion. Perhaps these new modes of communication seem unquestionably valuable; possibly they simply seem inevitable. But we think the questions need to be asked.

The fact that no one knows what the results of our experiments in virtuality will be does not discourage people from making predictions. Here are two visions of the effects of new communication technology, remarkable in their similarities and differences. One comes from Marshall MacLuhan and Quentin Fiore in the 1960s:

> *Electric circuitry has overthrown the regime of "time" and "space" and pours upon us instantly and continuously the concerns of all other men. It has reconstituted dialogue on a global scale. Its message is Total Change, ending psychic, social, economic, and political parochialism. . . . The new electronic interdependence recreates the world in the image of a global village.*[1]

A few events in part support the idea of the global village. Many believe that television images of the Vietnam War which brought the death and destruction of that distant conflict into people's homes built opposition that helped end it; television coverage of floods and famines at least temporarily turns the world's attention to disaster areas and stimulates sympathy and aid; images of students facing tanks in Tiananmen Square made China's social struggles a global issue. In general, though, events have discredited MacLuhan's belief that television and other innovations in communication and transportation destroy parochialism. What we know about how social capital develops helps us understand why information about the concerns of others does not automatically help us understand them, much less ensure that we will enter into mutually supportive relationships with them and become neighbors in a global village. (MacLuhan also seems to ignore the parochialisms that can divide traditional villages.) But the growth of the World Wide Web has revived MacLuhanesque ideas: of thriving electronic communities whose members may not know or care where their electronic companions live, of totalitarian regimes undermined by their inability to control information, of one giant human brain, global collaboration, and hopes for a "society that could advance with intercreativity and group intuition rather than conflict as the basic mechanism," in the words of Tim Berners-Lee, the Web's creator.[2]

The opposing view finds early and extreme expression in E. M. Forster's story "The Machine Stops," written about 100 years ago.[3] The story features a startlingly prescient description of a kind of World Wide Web that allows people all over the globe to see and hear one another and get easy access to all the world's information. Forster shows us people living in solitary chambers all over the world, electronically interdependent, as in MacLuhan's description, but totally isolated, so accustomed to a life of exchanging ideas only through the "Machine" that they develop "a horror of direct experience." They no longer travel or touch one another (except when required to for officially mandated procreation); most have lost all interest in the physical world, which they consider vulgar and devoid of "ideas."

It is probably safe to say that neither of these visions of the future describes the life we will live in twenty or fifty years, and that most other predictions about the effects of technology will prove wrong, as they always have. How new technologies will be used usually becomes apparent only when they are no longer new. The radio was expected to be used mainly for point-to-point communication, as its original name of "wireless telegraph" suggested. Late-nineteenth-century futurists imagined that the telephone, not the radio, would bring concerts to people's homes. And social expectations about the new technology of telephony in the 1880s were every bit as utopian as the most optimistic hopes for the Internet expressed today. Some believed then that the telephone would eliminate war: If kings, kaisers, presidents, and czars could speak directly to one another, free of the distorting intermediation of diplomats, permanent peace would be inevitable.[4] The early days of commercial television brought with them similarly optimistic claims that the new medium would elevate the level of political discourse and the cultural sophistication of the citizenry. No one predicted sound-bite news and programs like *Gilligan's Island*, *When Good Pets Go Bad*, and *Who Wants to Marry a Millionaire*? Descriptions of television as the new household "hearth" that would bring families together failed to anticipate a TV in every bedroom and a cable channel for every taste.

We have no right to feel superior to these discredited futurists of the past. Only five or six years ago, commentators argued that the Internet culture's prohibition against commercial exploitation of the medium would prevent businesses from using it, and their opinions were taken seriously. In retrospect, we can hardly believe that anyone in his right mind could have expected that fragile taboo to withstand the pressure of commercial and consumer interests.

The ways that technology will change society and work are even harder to imagine than how they will be used. We suspect that today's important new technologies will spur both less and more change than anticipated: less than those who predict a revolution in human behavior and a total transformation of society, more than those who view the latest innovation as a fad that will die as soon as people come to their senses, or survive only in a small, safe corner of our familiar world. Despite high hopes in some quarters, no invention has yet eliminated misunderstanding, suspicion, war, prejudice, or the need for human contact. On the other hand, inventions like the automobile and telephone have influenced society more deeply and broadly than anyone could have guessed when they appeared on the scene.

We are operating at a considerable disadvantage here, trying to draw conclusions about an experiment very much in process. Recognizing that it is an experiment has value in itself as an antidote to the people both "for" and "against" the new technology who claim to know more than anyone can. Within the context of our admitted uncertainty, we think it is possible to have a useful discussion of the relationship between virtuality and social capital.

Virtual Social Capital?

In this book, we have emphasized traditional means of building community, trust, loyalty, and membership—the traditional elements of social capital. We especially recommend conversation, storytelling, working side by side to build trust and mutual understanding, and meeting in social spaces over time as principal social capital investments. The social and psychological realities of how people work justify that emphasis. One lesson of this book is that reducing or interfering with those activities will likely reduce social capital and, in turn, reduce the stability and effectiveness of the organization. Many of our references to new communications technologies and related new ideas of the organization—the virtual organization, free agency—have been cautionary, warning of the damage they may do to social capital. We want to look at some of these issues a little more closely here. For one thing, the use of technology to link teams, practices, and other groups over distance—what we are calling "virtuality"—is a reality in many organizations today and may be even more common tomorrow. Second, the effects of virtuality are not all bad, provided that they are integrated into a balanced approach that takes the real requirements of building social capital into account. Finally, both new technologies and many of their uses will be different in the future. Some of the problems we describe will fade; new problems will certainly appear.

The Pros and Cons of Virtual Connections

E. M. Forster's short story anticipates today's concerns about people spending more and more time alone in front of a computer monitor or TV screen, shopping online, talking online, living online, mesmerized by information about the world or about the imaginary world of TV Land, "connected" but alone. In 1950 David Riesman titled his book of social commentary *The Lonely Crowd*. Today we worry more about "crowded solitude"—people awash in information about the outside world, but essentially cut off from their fellow human beings, both isolated and intruded upon—the worst of both worlds. This is the future Forster imagines. In a similar vein, Neil Postman challenges what he considers loose talk about Internet "communities" and e-mail "conversations" in *Building a Bridge to the Eighteenth Century*:

> A community is made up of people who may not have similar interests but who must negotiate and resolve their differences for the sake of social harmony. Tocqueville used the phrase "an ethic of reciprocity" to delineate what is at the heart of community life. What has that to do with "a community" of Internet users? As for "conversation," two (or more) people typing messages to each other are engaged in an activity quite different from what is usually called a conversation. To call messages that lack the presence of the human voice and human faces a "conversation" seems odd to me.[5]

Postman's sense of "community" and "conversation" is a lot like ours, rich in social capital and its signals, connections and commitments. We agree that calling the people who exchange messages on a Beanie Baby Web site a "community" depreciates the concept. Such a group mostly lacks the complex web of mutual adjustment and reciprocity that characterizes communities. Nevertheless, real social connection does happen online and should not be dismissed. Describing his participation in the WELL (Whole Earth 'Lectronic Link), Howard Rheingold convincingly chronicles genuine social connection via this famous example of what he calls "computer-mediated social groups." Participants in the WELL share laughter, grief, rage, and concerns about sick children and engage in collective efforts to help members in trouble.[6] It would be foolish and pedantic to deny that "WELLites" belong to a kind of community, one less intimate and committed than traditional communities in some senses but more so in others. The closeness of people who band together on the Web to share experiences of rare illnesses, the friendships and romances that begin as e-mail exchanges, and in general the rebirth of social writing thanks to the Internet all attest to the potential social power of online communication. Many Web community members point to opportunities to share thoughts and feelings that online communities sometimes provide more readily than "real" communities. We should avoid the mistake of measuring the genuine limitations of virtual communities against the imagined perfections of some ideal traditional one.

Rather than focus entirely on the alienating dangers of technology, we can sometimes marvel at how readily the human genius for connection socializes the seemingly cold machinery of keyboards and modems. The groups of young teenage girls who use America Online's Instant Messenger feature to "chat" together have developed a jargon shorthand that overcomes some of the limitations of typing and, like other jargons, reinforces social cohesion among those who know and use it. "Brb" (be right back), "g2g" (got to go), and "lol" (laughing out loud) are parts of a new keyboard language that makes their exchanges faster, more expressive, more conversational, and more intimate.[7]

If talking about e-mail "conversations" fails to do complete justice to what that word should mean, Postman's implied definition of a conversation seems unnecessarily narrow. Most of us believe that telephone conversations are real conversations, though they lack the presence of human faces he seems to require. A phone call may be less meaningful and satisfying than a long tête-à-tête over dinner, but it would be silly to deny that over time the phone has become one of the legitimate tools of human conversation.

In other words, we think that Postman goes too far in rejecting the idea of an Internet community, but we also think that he has a point. We believe that the technology available today is generally not an effective social medium and that *relying* on it for community, connection, and understanding—for social capital—is a mistake. Given the current state of technology, there are basic problems with virtuality, as stated below.

- None of the technology of virtuality can (currently) carry even a fraction of the whole range of communications that people use to relate to one another and that build social capital.

- Virtual connections (and the attention we give them) tend to be brief and intermittent; durable social connections and social-capital building take time.

- Virtual connections tend to have a clear, limited purpose (usually information exchange on a particular subject) and consciously chosen and limited participants; social connections more often grow from chance encounters and broad-ranging conversation and chat.

- Virtual communication such as e-mail and videoconferencing may actually distract people from what is going on around them so that they are, in effect, "neither here nor there."

For all these reasons and especially because of the loss of richness, breadth, and nuance, online is not yet the same as being there. Think of the difference between, on the one hand, experiencing a foreign country by living in it for a year and, on the other, by phoning friends who live there and looking at the photographs and souvenirs they send. Being there means taking in literally millions of impressions—sights, sounds, smells, tastes, and all the subtle details of behavior that are difficult to describe in words or even consciously notice but that gradually create a "feel" for the culture (and even, sometimes, an ability to adopt it and pass for a local). No secondhand reports or electronic windows on another part of the world can begin to duplicate that learning. If virtual tours were as good as the real thing, no one would bother to travel.

It is tempting but misleading to build a neat communication-richness hierarchy with e-mail at the low end of the scale (written words only, asynchronous communications), followed by telephone (words with inflections, immediate give-and-take), followed by video-conferencing (spoken words and images together), and face-to-face meeting (as full a range of sound, sight, and smell as we can discern, and the possibility of touch). Our experiences of these modes of communication are not that simple, though. E-mail has the advantage of a written record that allows participants to reflect on earlier parts of the "conversation." Telephone conversations are more ephemeral, but richer in expression. Though the absence of visual information sometimes causes awkwardness and misunderstanding, phones often provide a better means of communication than videoconferencing, perhaps because the phone is so reliable and familiar. We have had decades to learn how to use the telephone (though we are not yet sure how to handle the recent development of multiparty calls, where those not speaking tend to "disappear.") In other words, a whole range of factors come into play: how good the technology is; what the goals of the communication are; how many people are participating; how comfortable users are with it. We should keep in mind that some but not all of the problems of virtuality stem from its newness more than from inherent limitations. It takes time to learn what new technologies are really good for and to develop the social habits that make them a "natural" and appropriate part of how people relate. British Petroleum, one of the earliest successful practitioners of virtual teamwork supported by videoconferencing and shared computer programs, has developed protocols for entering and leaving multiparty electronic conversations to counter the problem of people invisibly signing on and off. A developing etiquette of virtual communication will undoubtedly make it more effective.

One of the things we are in the process of learning is the appropriate match of technology to task. Sloan School professor Wanda Orlikowski urges us not to think of rich, multimedia communication as automatically better than e-mail but to ask first, "What do we need to accomplish with this communication?" E-mail may be the most efficient and effective way to communicate straightforward information, but it is totally inadequate for building trust relationships or for complex negotiation or making decisions in ambiguous situations.[8] Relying on e-mail or Web-based meeting places to create trust and community is a mistake, we believe, though those things may help keep an existing community together. Using teleconferencing for a weekly sales update makes sense in many instances. Using it to make important decisions can be disastrous, even deadly, as the following example shows.

Limitations of Virtuality:
The *Challenger* Launch Decision

Diane Vaughan's deservedly praised painstaking analysis of NASA's *Challenger* launch decision dramatically illustrates some of the pitfalls of long-distance, technology-mediated communication.[9] The participants in the Flight Readiness Review that led to the tragically wrong decision to launch the space shuttle in cold weather in January 1986 were at three locations: the Kennedy Space Center in Florida, the Marshall Space Flight Center in Alabama, and a Morton Thiokol facility in Utah. They "met" via teleconferencing to evaluate the risk of a cold-weather launch, so they could hear but not see one another. In broad outline, this is what happened. Basing their judgment on somewhat ambiguous information from earlier flights, Morton Thiokol engineers raised doubts about the safety of the O-ring-sealed joints of the booster rockets. Larry Mulloy of the Marshall Center responded, "My God, Thiokol, when do you want me to launch, next April?" and Marshall's deputy director of science and engineering, George Hardy, said he was "appalled" by the Thiokol recommendation. Thiokol "went off-line" for half an hour and then came back to announce that they withdrew their opposition. The shuttle was launched; the O-rings failed, causing an explosion. The shuttle crashed and the crew died.

Vaughan's re-creation of the meeting shows how impoverishing the loss of nonverbal signals can be, and how much misunderstanding and disconnection can result when some of the dimensions of face-to-face communication are missing. As she notes,

"[C]ommunication between settings depended entirely on words, inflection, and silences, for many visual cues that normally aid interpretation—such as gestures, facial expressions, body posture, activity—were unavailable."[10] The critical missing gestures and expressions were not only those of the speakers, but of others in the three locations with them. The context of the responses and reactions of everyone involved disappears in a teleconference; in fact, people not actively engaged in the conversation seem to disappear altogether. All that the participants had to go on were a few disembodied voices and a few faxed charts. As a result, not only the nuances of the conversation but some of its central meaning failed to come across. The Morton Thiokol engineers missed the signs of Mulloy's and Hardy's uncertainty and willingness to listen. According to Vaughan,

> In fascinating testament to the power of visual information, [none of the team members] who were with Hardy at Marshall, perceived his comments as pressure. They could see him [with] ". . . his sleeves rolled up" . . . "working hard to understand" . . . and heard statements that did not carry over the network to Utah and the Cape ("For God's sake, don't let me make a dumb mistake" and Hardy's conversation . . . about phone calls to cancel the launch). Those opposed to the launch who were in the same setting as Hardy had more information that altered their interpretation.[11]

Moreover, when the Thiokol group withdrew its objections to launch, Mulloy and Hardy had no knowledge of the process that led to that change (including their own powerful influence on the process), and the continuing uncertainty and disagreement at Thiokol.

In addition to not carrying essential signals, the "distancing" technology of the telephone led to uncharacteristic behavior that exacerbated the problems. Vaughan tells us that social awareness moderates face-to-face Flight Readiness Reviews; the meetings are still adversarial, but people temper the harshness of their disagreements when they see real people across the table who might be enraged or humiliated by an all-out attack and are aware of their emotional reactions. With those people invisible, Mulloy and Hardy spoke more aggressively than they would have if everyone sat in the same room; their "opponents" perceived their comments as aggressive and definitive and interpreted them as almost irresistible pressure to approve a launch. A similar lack of social context and the invisibility of the recipient encourage e-mail attacks ("flaming") that would never occur in person. Geoff Mulgan comments on this phenomenon in *Connexity*:

> When communication shifts even further from face-to-face conversation towards text-based messages over electronic networks, one of the consequences is that people become less polite and less sensitive. There is more anger and indiscretion, more of the communicational equivalents of road rage.[12]

The limitations of NASA's virtual meeting both changed what people said and made it difficult to interpret their words. Vaughan's re-creation of the teleconference beautifully illustrates the complexity of effective communication and the social context of understanding, the ways that everything from status to tone to facial expression to whether or not someone has his sleeves rolled up contributes to our ability to know what other people mean and so work together effectively. The *Challenger* decision example shows why the technology of virtuality is still inadequate for the complex and delicate work of negotiation, developing mutual understanding, and dealing with ambiguous information.

Vaughan's emphasis on the damaging lack of visual cues suggests that a videoconference could have worked better, and might even have changed the outcome. That possibility does not negate the general point that the loss of the richness of close communication endangers understanding and trust. This is true for videoconferencing too, at least in its current state of development, when poor image quality and poorly synchronized image and sound mask and distort signals of social meaning. It is still no substitute for being there. Disney's Michael Eisner, not generally known as a consensus builder, makes the point well:

> Sometimes you just have to be there with your people. You have to be in the same room with them, look them in the eyes, hear their voices. I'll tell you one thing. Most of the bad decisions I've made, I've made while teleconferencing. In creative companies, you have to be able to read body language—see the look in people's eyes when an idea is launched, see whether they fall asleep.[13]

Telecommuting and Its Discontents

Telecommuting has not grown nearly as fast as some commentators have expected. Futurist Alvin Toffler predicted a world of nearly deserted traditional offices as employees shipped their work electronically from whatever pleasant places they chose to live; others anticipated that more than half of all workers in the United States would work from home by the year 2000.[14]

The fact that these predictions have proved so spectacularly wrong reflects the limitations of the technology of virtuality that we discuss here and, more broadly, the inherent socialness of work. Imagining that more than half the working population of the United States would even want to work alone at home reveals a startling disregard for people's social needs and ignores the role of social capital in the workplace. Cheerleading for telecommuting reflects two assumptions, both wrong: that most work (even or especially knowledge work) is individual, and that technology creates adequate social connections.

As we suggested earlier, even tasks that seem ideally suited to the worker alone in his home usually have important social components that the official organization and the categories of process analysis usually fail to recognize. The health insurance claims processors that Etienne Wenger vividly and precisely describe in *Communities of Practice* seem to be good candidates for telecommuting.[15] Each processor has a computer and telephone and a daily quota of claims to be processed. Why not save real estate costs and enlarge the pool of potential employees by farming the work out to individuals in home offices? Wenger's detailed analysis shows how very social even this work is. Everyone in the claims processing office has her own desk and her own stack of claims to process, but people quite frequently interact, asking each other questions about ambiguous situations, overhearing conversations that give them information they need, jointly recalling past situations to help them interpret new ones. Newcomers learn shortcuts and subtleties from experienced workers that training courses never teach because the official organization does not know them. The more purely social elements of the day—lunch and breaks, opportunities to celebrate and commiserate together—help define acceptable behaviors and create a sense of belonging that contributes to effective work. What is true of health insurance claims processing is clearly true of most service and knowledge jobs: the work and the workers depend on social connection, both because of the limitations of technology and some irreducible facts about the socialness of human beings.

Here is another important but often ignored point: Some people are innately more social than others. Essential questions of personality type need to be taken into account. Some people are happy and productive working mainly alone, but they are probably a very small minority. Our unscientific, anecdotal observation is that most of the people who think they would enjoy working at home seldom do for long. It is easy to imagine and for a while easy to enjoy the pleasure of giving up rush-hour drives; the loneliness of being away from the life of the office is harder to anticipate in advance. Many who try telecommuting and many companies they work for change their minds about the efficacy of working at home. Brown and Duguid refer to a telecenter study that shows 25 percent of telecommuters returning to the office within five months and 50 percent within a year.[16]

Many organizations and some hundreds of thousands of people use telecommuting (estimates vary depending on how work at home is defined), some successfully. It is part of the experiment-in-progress in virtuality and can help us identify some problems and possibilities.

The main arguments in its favor are these:

- for the telecommuter, avoiding long daily trips to and from the office and increased opportunities for time-shifting to balance the demands of work and personal life;

- for the organization, access to the talents of workers unable or unwilling to work regular hours in an office and possible savings on facilities (though the cost of equipment and support for telecommuters may reduce or eliminate those savings).

The social capital costs of telecommuting often outweigh these advantages. We have described how the rituals and daily activities of organizational life create community, define and reinforce norms and values, build trust and shared understanding, help define identities, and provide the intangible rewards of recognition and fellowship that are such an important part of work. First and most obviously because telecommuters are rarely at the office, they are cut off from the life of the office and the benefits it provides.

At least in its current state of development, the technology of virtual work cannot bridge the gap between the worker at home and the office. Like the individual who tries to take part in a foreign culture through phone calls and photographs rather than by being immersed in the culture, the telecommuter experiences the life of the workplace mainly at secondhand.

Even the relatively richer forms of online communication—video-conferencing, for instance—tend to be too purposeful and information oriented, and no substitute for the communication, especially the social communication, that flows continually through the work-place. Coworkers define and redefine who they are as a group in part by sharing and monitoring reactions to events at work, news of the outside world, weather, the behavior of bosses and subordi-nates, and the thousands of other subjects that form the currency of daily communication. They solidify and redefine group mem-bership, strengthening connections in hundreds of small ways and making new connections, often by chance. Telecommuters have fewer opportunities to tend and expand their personal networks. They are excluded from the accidental meetings that occur in the cafeteria or the unanticipated conversations with a new employee or a customer who happens to be on site that may uncover mutual interests. They also learn less. A Department of Labor study based on extensive research at eight large U.S. firms showed that at least 80 percent of workplace learning occurs informally—but you have to be there to take advantage of it. Experience shows that telecommuters also suffer the effects of the out-of-sight-out-of-mind syndrome, get-ting less credit for their work and fewer opportunities for interesting new work than employees who happen to be on the spot when something comes up. The chances for advantageous serendipity go way down for telecommuters.

Telecommuting tends to reduce the rich web of connections that make an individual part of an organization to a fragile few. Coher-ence and cooperation are likely victims. The telecommuter knows less about what goes on, who is doing the work, and how it is being done. Loyalty also suffers. If telecommuting mainly means receiving information and assignments online and e-mailing responses and results back, what binds an individual to one company rather than another? If a telecommuter can earn a few dollars more by e-mailing similar work to a different address, what prevents her from changing jobs whenever a marginally better offer comes along?

In "Two Cheers for the Virtual Office," Tom Davenport and Keri Pearlson point to some of these threats to social capital. They cite a Cornell study of IBM virtual office workers, 77 percent of whom judged that "professional communication at work" was somewhat or much worse than when they worked in the office and 88 percent of whom said that their ability to socialize with coworkers was worse or much worse.[17] Some companies and individuals discover that the drawbacks of telecommuting outweigh the advantages and move back to more traditional arrangements; the migration of tele-center workers back to the office, mentioned earlier, is one example.

A few companies have instituted programs to mitigate some of the negative aspects of telecommuting. Davenport and Pearlson mention one consumer products company that discourages anyone who has been with the organization for less than a year from working at home, because they recognize the need for new employees to absorb the culture of the firm and make connections with a variety of people. Hewlett-Packard has developed a program for managers of remote workers that deals with communication, leadership, and evaluation issues, and NCR has coaches to help virtual teams work together. It is telling, by the way, that these HP managers and NCR teams regularly meet face-to-face to confront the problems of working at a distance. Probably the best way to limit the negative effects of working at a distance is not to do it all the time.

With an understandable interest in virtual work for itself and its customers, British Telecom has begun to look at the question of how to connect mobile (and even nomadic) workers with one another. BT uses what it calls "mobility leaders" to help create community, build alliances, and foster relationships in a world of work that extends across national and organizational borders and is always on the move. They have come to believe that an aptitude for connecting with others is the glue needed to hold organizations together in an era of interdependence and dispersed, shifting enterprises—the "NQ"—network intelligence—that Tom Boyle talks about. He sees a shift in knowledge management focus from collecting documents to making connections between people.

BT is also trying to develop technology that helps "retap the oral tradition," in Boyle's words.[18] The firm is working on voice-to-text applications that can allow individuals to record thoughts and impressions in a (somewhat) natural way while they are still fresh—for instance, while driving from a work site. The idea is to give shareable information naturalness and immediacy, while circumventing people's reluctance to use the keyboard. If this kind of effort succeeds in making electronic communication more natural, it will probably be beneficial, but only if it does not replace more direct contact.

In any case, these measures are steps in the right direction or at least demonstrate a recognition of important issues. In themselves, they cannot make up for the losses that telecommuting and the dispersion of organizations into lone road warriors create. Chuck Sieloff of Hewlett-Packard worries that an increase in telecommuting may gradually erode the company's social capital, undermining the organization's shared understanding of the HP way and weakening the behaviors that helped make the firm successful for so long.

Social Capital and the Web

Kennedy School of Government professor Jane Fountain, who studies the Internet and social capital, says that the absence of norms and trust—essential components of social capital—are the greatest barriers to using the Internet as a tool for building social capital. The openness of the Web is one of its defining strengths, but the fact that anyone can use it makes it impossible to agree to norms of behavior or enforce them (hence the ongoing struggle over what to do about hate groups and pornography on the Web). The ease with which almost anyone can construct a professional-looking Web site makes it hard to judge whether you are dealing with a reputable institution that can back up its promises, a fly-by-night operation, or a single con man.

People can obviously be fooled in person too, but it is harder to do. We judge others by words and tone, by how they move and how they dress, by the "vibrations" they seem to give off, by how they respond to situations over time, and by how other people respond to them and talk about them. Many of these signals are missing in the relatively flat online environment. The fact that online contacts tend to be brief and focused on a particular aim or transaction makes it easier to maintain a false front and harder to detect one.

Web founder Berners-Lee recognizes these difficulties and the importance of trying to resolve them when he talks about "fundamental socio-technical issues that could make or break the Web." He explains that "[t]hese have to do with information quality, bias, endorsement, privacy, and trust—fundamental values in society, much misunderstood on the Web, and also highly susceptible to exploitation by those who can find a way."[19]

Glen Urban, former dean of the MIT Sloan School of Management, has been exploring ways of creating trust on the Web, applying learning about how people come to trust others to the design and management of Web environments. So, for instance, because we are more likely to trust people who make their personal stake in a business clear (our familiar trust/transparency connection), he recommends that trust-based commercial Web sites be explicit about how they make their money.

Unfortunately, we already see examples of online entities squandering trust by disguising or misrepresenting their sources of income. Amazon.com, certainly one of the best-known brand names on the Web and seemingly a pioneer in developing a trust relationship with its customers, provides a case in point. Among the "services" Amazon.com offered customers were recommendations of good new books, like the tips that a book-loving bookshop owner shares with her discriminating readers. Word that publishers could buy this prime recommendation space damaged the developing trust relationship between bookseller and reader. There are also the teenagers paid by music publishers (often in the currency of CDs and concert tickets) to talk up a band or a new recording in online chats. Interestingly, genuine (unpaid) fans have begun to recognize these shills by their slightly overinsistent harping on the wonderfulness of a particular performer. Sites have also come under fire for selling personal information it gathers from users. The relationship-building promised by Web contacts between companies and customers is threatened by this practice, just as personal relationships are threatened when one party uses information about the other for his own advantage. The technology company head recently quoted as saying "Privacy is dead, get used to it," underestimates the power of the human desire for privacy and autonomy. A national drugstore chain that sold medical information about customers to pharmaceutical firms (supposedly so customers could enjoy the advantage of receiving relevant information about new drugs) got a small sample of this power in the form of widespread, vociferous outrage and quickly abandoned the scheme.

Even within organizations where norms can generally be maintained and some initial, provisional trust of others probably exists, trust is harder to keep alive through electronic connections than through face-to-face contact, according to one study. Highest at the beginning of these electronic collaborations, trust declines as soon as members' expectations of others are disappointed. Especially in large organizations, where people may not have contact apart from their electronic exchanges, neither a preexisting foundation of trust or knowledge of the collaborators apart from their participation in the project is available to moderate their disapproval.

A Repertoire of Connections

A few virtual groups have collaborated successfully online without ever meeting in person. Most or all of these seem to be software development groups. (The online development of the Linux operating system is an example, and members of Xerox's Common Management Interface software group have never met face-to-face). Hal Varian, dean of the School of Information Management and Systems at the University of California at Berkeley, believes that software development particularly lends itself to electronic collaboration because good software tends to be modular and because the people who write software tend to be comfortable in an electronic environment. He adds, however, that such virtual development processes seem to require a charismatic leader to hold them together.[20]

In general, though, successful virtual work depends on using a broad repertoire of kinds of connection, communication, and cooperation to build the trust and understanding that collaboration requires. Global consulting firms and other dispersed organizations that support community development for collaboration and knowledge exchange generally recognize or have discovered from bitter experience that electronic communication alone does not create either community or collaboration. Many organizations find that people must meet in person to begin to cohere into a group and then have periodic meetings to reconnect and recalibrate their shared understanding and commitment. In these cases, electronic communication and face-to-face meetings support each other: the mutual engagement of a living community encourages members to answer electronic requests for help and contribute to a shared system; valuable shared content and an active online discussion connect people and can motivate them to contact people directly.

When Mike Burtha became head of knowledge networking at Johnson & Johnson in 1997, he looked for a project that could quickly succeed and demonstrate the value of building virtual communities among the 170 companies in fifty countries that comprised the company.[21] He discovered that more than 150 people were working on the Y2K problem—working in ways very similar to children engaged in parallel play on the playground, aware of each other and yet keeping to themselves, not quite figuring out how to get together. Because their work was so similar, Burtha thought that he could organize them into a knowledge-sharing community. He built a well-designed electronic chat room, expecting that the obvious advantages of exchanging Y2K information would certainly draw them to it. They did not come, because they were not yet a community and the existence of the chat room could not make them one. Only Burtha's considerable efforts—prodding, discussing, encouraging, cajoling—began to help those individuals become a group. That active human agency was required to jump-start the community.

Modern high-energy physics experiments offer a striking example of what it takes to enable (partly) virtual work groups to carry out complex tasks together. Physicist Tim Kinnel has written about the importance of using a broad range of connection and communication techniques in these huge collaborations (of as many as 2,000 scientists from well over 100 institutions).[22] Meeting in person is essential, especially at the critical planning and analysis stages of the work. Both the initial need to build trust and consensus—to create community—and the later intense and far-ranging analytical discussions of complex results call for a face-to-face meeting. Kinnel comments, "This investment of time and money in travel points up the vital importance of personal contact to successful collaboration, despite the ubiquity of various communications technologies." The virtual connections that help hold the group together during experiments which can easily last more than a decade involves a whole range of technologies: e-mail for frequent exchanges of pieces of information, Web sites for papers and larger information "chunks," and videoconferencing for virtual meetings when explanation and discussion are required. Kinnel says that "a mix of successful communications techniques has been the key to successful communication," and quotes Wesley Smith, a member of one of the largest collaborations:

> I see the guys at CERN [European Organization for Nuclear Research] once about every six weeks or a month. . . . But then I also see them once a week over video and that way we keep connected and keep up to date on things. And then of course, there's tons of e-mail flying back and forth now. It's that combination of e-mail, once in a while a phone call (although fairly rare), videoconferencing, and going there that makes it work.[23]

Not all collaborative work requires this rich a mixture of meeting and technology, but the example does suggest how the technology of virtuality can support and even enhance the social capital such work requires when that technology is part of a wider context of working together and is used appropriately.

Who Organizes the Virtual Organization?

The feasibility of the virtual organization—that all-star group assembled to take advantage of a particular opportunity—is limited partly by the limits of technology we have discussed. Since trust and understanding are nearly impossible to develop and difficult to maintain at a distance, organizations that are networks of individuals held together by technology will have a hard time acting coherently and cooperatively. The problem is exacerbated when newly formed and temporary groups do not have a preexisting set of

norms, goals, values, and understandings to fall back on and to provide a supportive and explanatory context for their virtual dealings.

In *Living on Thin Air*, knowledge consultant and adviser to the
British government Charles Leadbeater rehearses the arguments in
favor of the virtual organization—their hoped-for responsiveness,
flexibility, and freedom from the dead weight of hierarchies—and
then goes on to say that the reality is different from that optimistic
theory:

> *Dispersed, networked organizations take a great deal of patient management.
> They only work with a strong sense of common values and rules. If an orga-
> nization becomes too decentralized it will find it difficult to take concerted
> action when needed. A virtual organization often needs a smaller yet
> stronger centre. The best organizations are both networked and integrated.
> The key corporate skill is not simply to network but to integrate the diverse
> sources of knowledge and input provided by a network. If a company does
> not have strong core capabilities it will find itself dissolving into its net-
> work.*[24]

So why does the virtual organization model work in the film
industry? Mainly, we believe, because, although each film is different (well, most are), the *process* of making a film is pretty much
standardized—the "rules" are set, to use Leadbeater's word. Roles
are well defined. Everyone knows what the actors, electricians, foley
artists, gaffers, makeup artists, animal wranglers, drivers, and other
crew members are supposed to do. These processes are socially
embedded. Shared contexts, vocabularies, and legends abound.
Films vary and directors' approaches may differ to some extent,
but the craft of filmmaking is well defined. There is no single clear
"craft" of responding to a business opportunity or developing an
innovative new product, though. Each effort calls for negotiation
and definition of roles, aims, and the process of carrying out the
work. Also (and even taking into account struggles for power and
influence on the movie set), the filmmaking "organization" is not a
network of equals but a tightly structured hierarchy mobilized in
service of a director's or producer's vision.

Worth noting too is the fact that the people who gather to make
a film generally already belong to a close personal network. People
mainly hire the people they know and have worked with before.

This will probably also be true of the virtual corporations that do successfully form—the idea of a truly open system that finds the people whose talents exactly match the demands of a particular project, of recruiting a team over the Web, say, choosing people solely on the basis of ability, runs counter to human and organizational experience. In fact, the likelihood of success for virtual corporations depends even more on existing communities and connections than traditional organizations: the shared understanding, values, trust, and respect that successful work requires have to come from somewhere. In more traditional organizations, they can develop over time through the process of working together and with the guidance of strong leaders; for virtual organizations to work, they have to exist already, from past experiences of being together and working together.

The Persistence of Human Contact

The limited growth and occasional failures of telecommuting, the continuing unmistakable benefits of colocation (and people's continued willingness to put up with high prices, crowded highways, and the threat of earthquakes to be where the action is), and the paucity of verifiable examples of the virtual corporation in action all suggest that virtuality cannot (or not yet) support the social connection that people and organizations require. The clearest proof of the limitations of technology is the persistence of human contact. Studies show that communications technology may eliminate some face-to-face meetings, but in general, increased e-mail does not mean decreased travel. Instead, it contributes to the need and desire to meet with a broader range of people. Geoff Mulgan puts this phenomenon in a historical context:

> Throughout the twentieth century physical mobility and communications grew in tandem rather than as substitutes. The spread of the telephone accompanied that of commuter railways and trams, the radio accompanied the spread of cars and aeroplanes, the television that of motorways and jets, and everywhere the graphs of traffic movement move in parallel with the graphs of communication usage. In the same way, and contrary to common

sense, the consumption of electronic culture often generates demand for the real thing: as the UK's Open University discovered, the experience of distance learning increased demand for face-to-face learning."[25]

As our opening anecdote suggests, people still need to be there. Conference organizers promote their events by promising that such-and-such leading business speaker will actually be there to present the keynote address. (We have been at conferences where the advertised personality failed to appear or spoke by way of a video link. The disappointment and sometimes the anger of the audience are palpable.) Even Bay area members of the WELL, the online community mentioned earlier, meet in person for picnics and to work out the details of organizing new online discussion groups. If anything, the hunger to meet face-to-face, to see for yourself, to find out what your colleague or customer or partner is *really* like (and if they can really be trusted) is greater than ever. Also, the ease with which people can send messages to each other by e-mail or fax actually gives the face-to-face meeting extra value as a proof of commitment and attention. We believe that the persistence of face-to-face meeting reflects not just an old habit but some irreducible facts about how people form communities and collaborate.

The Balancing Act

What we said about volatility—that high social capital can help protect organizations from the damage it can cause—holds true for virtuality too. Organizations that have robust networks and communities, a deep reservoir of trust, and a clear sense of organizational identity are likely to have more success performing virtual work than organizations that are somewhat fragmented and likely to become more fragmented by trying to work at a distance. Russell Reynolds Associates has had considerable success sharing knowledge and work through its RRAccess global system and success bringing together teams from various offices because it built its virtual work on a foundation of trust and strong social ties (mostly formed in traditional ways). Perils of virtuality including lack of commitment to the organization, uncertainty about norms and values, low trust, misunderstanding, and even loneliness can be made less perilous by the grounding and connecting power of high social capital. It is also possible, though, that high social capital may temporarily mask damage caused by reliance on virtual work. Chuck Sieloff of Hewlett-Packard has expressed a concern that such organizations may embrace telecommuting and virtual teaming and not be aware that their stocks of social capital are being depleted until they suddenly find that organizational identity and coherence have been seriously eroded.

We make two recommendations. One is that organizations become aware of the potential social capital costs of telecommuting and other kinds of virtual work. Just as companies making decisions about hoteling or efficient space design should weigh savings against the social costs of their plans, organizations adopting virtual work practices should look at benefits and costs. Virtual connections, which can maintain and build ties under the right conditions, are a more complicated issue than hoteling, but a similar comparison of benefits and drawbacks should be possible. Applying the social capital management principle of "First do no harm" depends on knowing what kind of harm might occur when you make changes in how people work.

Many of the examples in this chapter suggest the second recommendation: that organizations keep virtuality in balance by employing a variety of ways of meeting and working together. Often, you have to be there: to hash out complicated decisions; to get to know the people you will be working with; to demonstrate commitment. Sometimes, an e-mail exchange or a videoconference will do. Most of the organizational communities that thrive—like that of the high-energy physicists—use the whole rich repertoire of face-to-face meeting and on-site work, e-mail, electronic work space, and video-conferencing to maintain their identities and work well together. Organizations as a whole similarly need to balance traditional and virtual ways of working to maintain *their* identities and cohesion.

We cannot predict the future of technology, but we think that this advice will hold firm, even as communications technology continues to develop. Some things will undoubtedly change. Many of the limitations we have mentioned—limitations on ease and naturalness of use but especially what we call limitations of "presence" caused by the relative poverty of electronic communication—are being addressed by technology improvements. We will not have to wait very long for communications technologies that make today's Internet and videoconferencing connections seem even more primitive than the first small gray television images look to us now. A recent *New York Times* article describes a distance learning experience involving the University of Wisconsin and two Japanese universities that features wall-size video to give students and teachers a sense of connection with participants at the other locations.[26] Though the picture quality is still not quite lifelike and sound-transmission delays create problems, the technology does provide more presence than small, jerky video. More important, it suggests a future when vastly improved technology will make virtual communication almost like being there. Several of the limitations we warn about in this chapter may decrease dramatically. We believe that a social capital perspective can help guide improvements in the technology itself and teach us how and when to use virtual technologies effectively. Understanding how trust and understanding develop, the life cycles of networks and communities, and the full meaning of conversation should help shape the future design of the machinery of virtual work.

Technical improvements may increase some problems. When communications technology becomes so much like "the real thing" that face-to-face meetings are widely considered an unnecessary and inefficient luxury, we may suffer social capital losses that we barely notice but that may accumulate into a new kind of aloneness—the loneliness of crowded solitude. Even life-size, 3-D images and CD-quality sound can leave us hungry for human connection. We do not expect E. M. Forster's nightmare world to come to pass, but the note of caution he sounded even before the seductive pseudo-reality of television came into existence is worth heeding. Paying attention to social capital will help balance the wilder claims of those who argue that technology can do everything, including transform humanity.

Virtual work is part of the world of the twenty-first century and we expect it will become an increasingly more important part. A social capital perspective can help us locate its proper place in the larger landscape of human connection and cooperation.

EPILOGUE

W<small>E HOPE THAT</small> the observations, examples, and advice that we have presented in this book strike you as sensible and even self-evident. As we said at the beginning, everyone who has ever worked in an organization (or gone to high school or belonged to a religious group or played on a team) already knows a great deal about how social capital is created and destroyed, and how important it is to all of our collective endeavors and our sense of self. We all know from experience that most of our achievement and satisfaction come through connections with other human beings. Not only our membership in families, teams, communities, and organizations, but the constant buzz of conversation that fills our days shows that we are social beings. Long before this book was published, most of us saw how much we work and play in groups and most of us understood the kinds of things that tend to bring us together or drive us apart, that encourage or inhibit cooperation. There is, for instance, nothing surprising about the idea that inviting people to participate increases their sense of belonging and willingness to contribute, or that failing to give them credit for their efforts tends to alienate and discourage them.

As we also have also noted, though, these common truths have gone largely unacknowledged, especially in organizations. They have been hidden by their very commonness, as well as by a mythology of independence and individuality and by management literature that has looked at organizations as machines, as clusters of processes, or as loose collections of individuals rather than as social organisms. Many organizations still operate on late-nineteenth or early-twentieth-century premises and principles, developed at a time when land, labor, and capital were considered the only sources of institutional wealth. The management tools that this assumption produced—most evident in the military and in railroad, steel, and mineral firms—were specifically designed to exploit those resources, not human and social resources as we are coming to understand them now. While those command-and-control mechanisms have become more sophisticated and complex, they still represent ways of managing the work of the nineteenth century. We need new models, metrics, and methods to help us grow and use the new sources of institutional and social wealth: knowledge and interdependence. We believe a social capital perspective can help shape those tools.

These issues are not entirely new. Terms like *goodwill, quality of life,* and even *culture* have long been used by commentators seeking answers to the questions of what an organization is really like and where its value resides. More recently, organizations including the World Bank, the United Nations, OECD, and the European Union have been developing indicators that include far more than per capita GNP to measure social capital specifically and get a handle on why a state, country, or global region works well—what makes it successful socially and economically. Applying the same kind of approach to organizations is generally still a new idea, many people still somehow believing that organizations are exempt from the social realities that govern the rest of life—even though evidence to the contrary greets them at their offices and factories every day. The new tools will come when that evidence is given its due.

A large part of our job here has been to speak unspoken obvious truths. We hope that the tour we have taken together, pointing out the social capital hidden in plain sight in organizations,

will help those organizations respect and nourish the human relationships that underlie so much of their current and future success. Even by themselves, awareness and respect will go a long way
to preserving and nurturing social capital in organizations. What
is noticed and valued tends to thrive, even without major programs and initiatives.

Without authentic respect for social capital, none of the interventions we describe will succeed. Remember, we are talking about
trust, relationship, and identity, and we human beings tend to know
when someone is trying to manipulate our feelings and judgments
about those core issues. Going through the motions of team building
or "visioning" cannot produce lasting social capital. One element of
authenticity is persistence. As trust builds over time, so we prove
our commitment over time: what we do day after day reveals what
matters most to us. And social capital, because it represents the
organic growth of trust, understanding, and loyalty, takes time to
develop. An American visitor to Oxford marveled at the smooth
green perfection of the lawn inside the quadrangle of one of Oxford
University's venerable colleges. While he stood admiring it, a
groundskeeper appeared through one of the entries. The visitor
asked him the secret of that lawn, so superior to any he had seen
in the United States. The groundskeeper said, "There's no secret.
Only soil, seed, water, and 500 years of rolling." It does not take anything like 500 years to build social capital in an organization, but it
does take consistent effort over time. There is no quick fix.

As we write these last paragraphs in the spring of 2000, the
newspapers we glance through in the morning feature articles about
how surprised some people are that various transforming trends in
business and society do not seem to be progressing as predicted.
The *Boston Globe* describes a Cambridge, Massachusetts, conference
on the Internet and Society in which Mitch Kapor, founder of
Lotus, describes himself as "a recovering technological utopian"
and confesses that the Internet is not simply going "to make everything better," as he once believed. At the same meeting, Harvard
president Neil Rudenstine says that online universities cannot equal
or replace the experience of being at a university. (Yes, he has a
vested interest in that view, but he is still right.)[1] A *New York Times*
article written in the aftermath of plunging stock prices for dot-com
companies (and the resulting restlessness of employees who are

coming up empty in the dot-com gold rush) suggests that loyalty matters after all. It praises Hewlett-Packard's long-standing policy of hiring people who fit the culture and companies including Cisco Systems and Southwest Airlines that work to make their workers valued participants. The article cites Harvard professor Charles O'Reilly, who says that "companies that keep workers well informed find that employees come to feel they have a stake in the company, even if they own only a little stock."[2]

None of this rediscovery of loyalty, respect, membership, and commitment surprises us. We hope, at this point, that it does not surprise the readers of In Good Company. The continued importance of those qualities has been our consistent theme.

The years ahead will no doubt bring exaggerated stories of transformation in organizations and society, as well as news of some genuinely significant changes in how we work and live. Peter Drucker, who has been a better predictor of the future of organizations than anyone else we can think of, said in 1998, "The nature of the organization will change. The corporation, the university, and the hospital will look as different from today's organizations thirty years from now as today's are different from those of 1890 or 1900."[3] We cannot guess what the organizations of 2028 will look like. We do know, though, that trust, community, connection, conversation, and loyalty will make them work and will make work meaningful for their members. The value of the social capital elements they embody will be rediscovered again and again because they lie at the heart of our humanness and our human ability—and need—to do things together.

NOTES

PREFACE

1. Sumantra Ghoshal and Christopher A. Bartlett, *The Individualized Corporation: A Fundamentally New Approach to Management* (New York: HarperBusiness, 1997).
2. Jonathan Kinghorn, "U-Turn at Unipart," *Knowledge Directions* 1, no. 1 (Fall 1999): 6–18.

CHAPTER 1

1. Information about United Parcel Service comes primarily from company interviews, UPS legacy books, and Jeffrey Sonnenfeld and Meredith Lazo's Harvard Business School case, "United Parcel Service (A)," Case 9-488-016 (Boston: Harvard Business School, 1987; rev. 1992).
2. "UPS Company of the Year," *Forbes*, 10 January 2000, 17–30.
3. Robert Putnam, "Bowling Alone: America's Declining Social Capital," *Journal of Democracy* 6, no. 1 (1995), 65–78.
4. Jane Jacobs, *The Decline and Rise of American Cities* (New York: Random House, 1961), 138.
5. Glenn Loury, "A Dynamic Theory of Racial Income Differences," in *Women, Minorities and Employment*, ed. P. A. Wallace and A. LeMond (Lexington, MA: Lexington Books, 1977).
6. See James Coleman, "Social Capital in the Creation of Human Capital," *American Journal of Sociology* 94 (1988): S95–S120 and

James S. Coleman, *Foundations of Social Theory* (Cambridge, MA: Harvard University Press, 1995).

7. The fullest sociological exposition of social capital comes from Ron Burt of the University of Chicago whose book *Structural Holes* (Cambridge, MA: Harvard University Press, 1993) is written, however, from a more individual perspective than we take in this book. A useful, up-to-date summary of sociological thinking on social capital written by Princeton University professor Alejandro Portes can be found in "Social Capital: Its Origins and Applications in Modern Society," *Annual Review of Sociology* 22 (1998): 1–24, and reprinted in Eric Lesser, ed., *Knowledge and Social Capital* (Boston: Butterworth-Heinemann, 2000), chapter 3.

8. A good example is Deepa Narayan, *Bonds and Bridges: Social Capital and Poverty* (Washington, D.C.: World Bank Poverty Division, 1999).

9. Michael Woolcock, "Social Capital and Economic Development: Towards a Theoretical Synthesis and Policy Framework," *Theory and Society* 27 (1998): 151–208.

10. Geoff Mulgan, *Connexity: Responsibility, Freedom, Business and Power in the New Century* (London: Vintage, 1998), 119.

11. Etienne Wenger, *Communities of Practice* (New York: Cambridge University Press, 1998).

12. Or, as social psychologist Robert Kahn joked, "rules, tools, and fools"—a formulation pointed out by Bob Sutton of Stanford.

13. An example from a leading pharmaceutical company shows how easily low social capital can trump theoretically efficient processes. A clear six-step process for gathering clinical data in one place and reviewing it in another took twenty steps in practice. Attempts to fix the problem with investments in improved technology failed. The real problem was that the clinicians did not trust or respect each other. The solution was to bring them together to discuss their joint work, a meeting that began to develop the necessary trust and connection. See Patricia Seemann and Don Cohen, "The Geography of Knowledge: From Knowledge Maps to the Knowledge Atlas," *Knowledge and Process Management: The Journal of Corporate Transformation* 4, no. 4 (1998): 106–122.

14. Mitchell Lee Marks and Philip H. Mirvis, *Joining Forces: Making One Plus One Equal Three in Mergers, Acquisitions, and Alliances* (San Francisco: Jossey-Bass, 1998).

15. Jane Fountain, "Social Capital: A Key Enabler," in *Investing in Innovation*, eds. Lewis Branscomb and James Keller (Cambridge, MA: MIT Press, 1998).

16. Robert Putnam, "The Prosperous Community," *American Prospect* 13 (1993): 35–42.

17. John Seely Brown, "A Conversation with John Seely Brown," interview by Don Cohen, *Knowledge Directions* 1 (Spring 1999): 32.

18. Dorothy Leonard, *Wellsprings of Knowledge* (Boston: Harvard Business School Press, 1995).

19. Arie de Geus, *The Living Company* (Boston: Harvard Business School Press, 1997), 82.

20. From Bob Sutton, who has made several valuable studies of the IDEO culture.

21. Erasmus (1465–1536) was supposedly the last person who did.

22. Some people have sold—and bought—the idea that information sources including the World Wide Web and company databases and intranets give each individual everything he needs to understand and carry out his work. This is and will remain untrue even as the Web becomes more pervasive and sophisticated. As numerous commentators have persuasively argued, learning and knowledge are socially situated. We learn and develop ideas mainly in communities; we draw useful material from the flood of information that threatens to overwhelm us by going to sources and interpreters we trust, by using our social world to select and filter.

23. From a presentation by Tom Boyle, a knowledge management consultant, at the Institute for Knowledge Management Member Forum, Nice, France, September 1999.

24. Powell spoke at the Berkeley Knowledge Forum, Berkeley, California, September 1997.

25. Sonnenfeld and Lazo, "United Parcel Service (A)."

26. John Seely Brown and Paul Duguid, *The Social Life of Information* (Boston: Harvard Business School Press, 2000).

27. Jim Kelly, CEO, United Parcel Service, interview by Don Cohen, Atlanta, GA, 26 January 2000.

28. The best and fullest current discussion of how these communities work is Etienne Wenger, *Communities of Practice*. See also Eric Lesser, ed., *Knowledge and Social Capital*.

29. See James Scott, *Seeing Like a State* (New Haven: Yale University Press, 1998) for a fuller exposition of this theme.

CHAPTER 2

1. Lisa Bernstein, "Opting Out of the Legal System: Extralegal Contractual Relations in the Diamond Industry," *Journal of Legal Studies* 21 (1992): 115–157.

2. Ibid., 157.

3. John L. Locke, *The De-Voicing of Society* (New York: Simon and Schuster, 1998), 110.

4. Kenneth J. Arrow, *The Limits of Organization* (New York: Norton, 1991).

5. See Francis Fukuyama, *Trust: The Social Virtues and the Creation of Prosperity* (London: Hamish Hamilton, 1995) and Debra Meyerson, Karl E. Weick, and Roderick Kramer, "Swift Trust in Temporary Groups," in *Trust in Organizations: Frontiers of Theory and Research*, eds. Roderick Moreland Kramer and Tom R. Tyler (Thousand Oaks, CA: Sage Publications, 1996).

6. Putnam, "Bowling Alone," 78.

7. Sztompka, *Trust: A Sociological Theory* (Cambridge: Cambridge University Press, 2000).

8. This point is made by Brian Uzzi in "Social Structure and Competition in Interfirm Networks: The Paradox of Embeddedness," *Administrative Science Quarterly* 42 (1997): 35–67 and in "Sources and Consequences for Economic Performance of Organizations: The Network Effect," *American Sociological Review* 61 (1996): 674–698.

9. Quoted in Locke, *The De-Voicing of Society*.

10. Putnam, "Bowling Alone," 21.

11. David Packard, *The HP Way: How Bill Hewlett and I Built Our Company* (New York: HarperBusiness, 1996), 135–136.

12. Ghoshal and Bartlett, *The Individualized Corporation*, 93.

13. Alice Early, Russell Reynolds Associates, interview by author (Cohen), New York City, 16 February 2000.

14. Quoted in Barbara Saidel and Don Cohen, "Collaboration at Russell Reynolds Associates: The Power of Social Capital," *Knowledge Directions* 2, no. 1 (Spring 2000): 6–22.

15. Hobson Brown Jr., President and CEO, Russell Reynolds Associates, interview by author (Prusak), New York City, Fall 1999.

16. Robert Axelrod, *The Evolution of Cooperation* (New York: Basic Books, 1984).

17. Karl E. Weick, *Sensemaking in Organizations* (Thousand Oaks, CA: Sage Publications, 1995), 145.

18. David Perkins and Daniel Wilson, "Bridging the Idea-Action Gap," *Knowledge Directions* 1, no. 2 (Fall 1999): 64–78.

19. AnnaLee Saxenian, *Regional Advantage: Culture and Competition in Silicon Valley and Route 128* (Cambridge, MA: Harvard University Press, 1996).

20. Brown and Duguid, *The Social Life of Information*.

21. Packard, *The HP Way*, 137.

22. Peter Drucker, "Managing Oneself," *Harvard Business Review* 77, no. 2 (March–April 1999): 72.

CHAPTER 3

1. Mark Walsh, CEO of VerticalNet, in a speech given at The Wharton Forum on Electronic Commerce, Philadelphia, PA, December 1999.

2. Uzzi, "Social Structure and Competition in Interfirm Networks," 64f.

3. Hendrik Flap, *Conflict, Loyalty and Violence: The Effects of Social Networks on Behavior* (New York: Peter Lang, 1988), 136.

4. George A. Hillery Jr., "Definitions of Community: Areas of Agreement," *Rural Sociology* 24 (1954): 111–124.

5. Raymond Williams, *Keywords: A Vocabulary of Culture and Society* (Oxford: Oxford University Press, 1987).

6. Wenger, *Communities of Practice*.

7. Francis Fukuyama, *The End of Order* (London: Social Market Foundation, 1997), 4.

8. For example, a more munificent nature, a sense of religious obligations, social striving through charitable display, and so on.

9. Malcolm Gladwell, "Six Degrees of Lois Weisberg," *The New Yorker*, 11 January 1999.

10. Mark Granovetter, *Getting a Job: A Study in Contacts and Careers*, 2nd edition (Chicago: University of Chicago Press, 1995).

11. Gladwell, "Six Degrees of Lois Weisberg."

12. Ibid., 60.

13. Susan Stucky, presentation to Ernst & Young Knowledge Consortium, New York City, 16 March 1993.

14. Brown, "A Conversation with John Seely Brown."

15. See *The Teaching Firm* (Newton, MA: Center for Workforce Department, 1998).

16. See Jean Lave and Etienne Wenger, *Situated Learning: Legitimate Peripheral Participation* (New York: Cambridge University Press, 1991).

17. Chris Argyris best explains this in his book *Knowledge for Action* (San Francisco: Jossey-Bass, 1993).

18. Quoted in Saidel and Cohen, "Collaboration at Russell Reynolds Associates," 6–22.

19. Julian Orr, *Talking About Machines: An Ethnography of a Modern Job* (Ithaca, NY: Cornell University Press, 1967), 60.

20. Ibid., 140.

21. An incident reported by Brian Hackett at a knowledge management discussion with British government officials attended by author (Cohen), New York, NY, April 1998.

22. See Thomas Davenport and Laurence Prusak, *Working Knowledge* (Boston: Harvard Business School Press, 1998).

23. See Brown and Duguid, *The Social Life of Information*.

24. Thomas J. Allen, *Managing the Flow of Technology* (Cambridge, MA: MIT Press, 1977).

25. Rob Cross, Andrew Parker, and Stephen P. Borgatti, "A Bird's-Eye View: Social Network Analysis for Knowledge Effectiveness," *Knowledge Directions* 2, no. 1 (Spring 2000): 48–62.

26. Information in this section is from Stephen Denning, World Bank, interviews with author (Prusak), and William Fulmer, "The World Bank and Knowledge Management," forthcoming Harvard Business School Case Study (Boston: Harvard Business School, 2000).

27. Steve Kerr, in a presentation at *Organization Science*'s Winter Conference, Keystone, CO, February, 2000.

28. John Seely Brown and Paul Duguid, "Practice vs. Process: The Tension That Won't Go Away," *Knowledge Directions* 2, no. 1 (2000): 86–96.

29. See Malcolm Gladwell, *The Tipping Point: How Little Things Can Make a Big Difference* (Boston: Little Brown & Company, 2000), 61–67.

30. Etienne Wenger, "Communities of Practice: The Key to Knowledge Strategy," *Knowledge Directions* (Fall 1999): 48–64.

31. Ibid.

32. This description of Chrysler's experience is drawn from Alvin Jacobson's study of Chrysler's development of its electronic book of knowledge, prepared for Ernst & Young's Center for Business Innovation in 1996.

33. A point Etienne Wenger makes in his writing on communities.

34. Stephen Denning, The World Bank, interview by author (Prusak), Washington, D.C., 5 August 2000.

Chapter 4

1. The story of the new Alcoa headquarters is taken from "Open for Business," *@Issue* 5, no. 2 (December 18, 1998), and from Peter Lawrence, chairman of the Corporate Design Foundation, interview by author (Cohen), Boston, MA, February 1999.

2. "Open for Business," 28.

3. Ibid., 26.

4. Ray Oldenburg, *The Great Good Place* (New York: Marlow & Co., 1997), p. xxviii.

5. Robin Dunbar, *Grooming, Gossip, and the Evolution of Language* (Cambridge, MA: Harvard University Press, 1996), 206.

6. Edward Verrall Lucas, *Wanderings and Diversions*, in *Bartletts Familiar Quotations* 1st edition, 725.

7. Brown and Duguid, *The Social Life of Information*, 70–73.

8. From an article by Philip Landon in the journal *Metropolis*, quoted in Tony Hiss, *The Experience of Place* (New York: Vintage Books, 1991), 18.

9. Oldenburg, *The Great Good Place*, xiv.

10. Quoted in Tony Hiss in *The Experience of Place* (New York: Vintage Books, 1990), 46.

11. Kinghorn, "U-Turn at Unipart," 12.

12. "Open for Business," 26.

13. Sim Sitkin, speaking during the Virtual Communities Workshop discussion at The Wharton School, Philadelphia, PA, 6 April 2000, as quoted by Don Cohen. This workshop was sponsored by the Reginald H. Jones Center and the Institute for Knowledge Management.

14. This comment was made at a Conference Board meeting on organizational learning, April 17–18, 1997, Chicago, IL.

15. Denise Rousseau, *Psychological Contracts in Organizations: Understanding Written and Unwritten Agreements* (Thousand Oaks, CA: Sage Publications, 1995), 149.

16. Quoted in Locke, *The De-Voicing of Society*, 104.

17. Jim Kelly, interview by Don Cohen.

18. Mulgan, *Connexity*, 98f.

CHAPTER 5

1. Lewis Thomas, *The Lives of a Cell* (New York: Viking, 1974), 112.

2. Robert D. Putnam, *Bowling Alone: The Collapse and Revival of American Community* (New York: Simon & Schuster, 2000).

3. Locke, *The De-Voicing of Society*, 18.

4. Ibid., 122.

5. Mulgan, *Connexity*, 96. Some others have argued that one's conversation with oneself is the fundamental unit of knowledge.

6. Theodore Zeldin, *Conversation* (London: Harville Press, 1998), 3.

7. Ibid., 53.

8. E. M. Forster, *Howards End* (New York: Book of the Month Club, 1995), 251.

9. Karl Sabbagh, *Twenty-First-Century Jet* (New York: Scribner, 1996), 36.

10. Locke, *The De-Voicing of Society*.

11. Discussed in Dunbar, *Grooming, Gossip, and the Evolution of Language*, 123.

12. Locke, *The De-Voicing of Society*, 104.

13. Brown and Duguid, *The Social Life of Information*, 102–103.

14. Packard, *The HP Way*, 157.

15. E. M. Forster, *Aspects of the Novel* (New York: Harcourt, Brace and World, 1954), 39.

16. Howard Gardner, *Leading Minds: An Anatomy of Leadership* (New York: Basic Books, 1995).

17. Stephen Denning, *The Springboard: How Storytelling Ignites Action in Knowledge-Era Organizations* (Boston: Butterworth-Heinemann, 2000).

18. Wendell Berry, *What Are People For?* (San Francisco: North Point Press, 1990), 157.

19. Elliot Mishler, *Storylines: Craftartists' Narratives of Identity* (Cambridge, MA: Harvard University Press, 1999), 19.

20. Gardner, *Leading Minds*, 43.

21. Brown and Duguid, *The Social Life of Information*, 106.

22. Gordon Shaw, Robert Brown, and Philip Bromiley, "Strategic Stories: How 3M Is Rewriting Business Planning," *Harvard Business Review* 76, no. 3 (May–June 1998): 50.

23. Many of the details of this well-known story and other aspects of 3M's organizational myths are taken from Ikujiro Nonaka and Hiro Takeuchi, *The Knowledge-Creating Company* (New York: Oxford University Press, 1995), 136–138.

24. Packard, *The HP Way*, 108.

25. Described by George Washington University professor Nancy Dixon at an Ernst & Young Center for Business Innovation working session, Boston, MA, 1997.

26. Orr, *Talking About Machines* 135.

27. All used as examples in Gardner, *Leading Minds*.

28. de Geus, *The Living Company*, 49.

29. Alanson Van Fleet, "Cultural Anthropology, Storytelling and Knowledge Management," *Knowledge Directions* 1, no. 1 (Fall 1999): 78–90.

30. Examples drawn from Sarah Getty, "Narrative Assets," *Knowledge Directions* 2, no. 1 (Spring 2000): 74–96.

31. Dorothy Leonard and Walter Swap, *When Sparks Fly* (Boston: Harvard Business School Press, 1999), 70.

CHAPTER 6

1. Alex Berenson, "In Silicon Valley, Loyalty Means Paying a High Price," *New York Times*, 28 May 2000, C1.

2. Quoted in Adrian Wooldridge, "Come Back, Company Man!" *New York Times Magazine*, 5 March 2000, 82.

3. Rob Cross, Director of Advanced Technologies, SAS Institute, phone interview by author (Cohen), 18 May 2000.

4. Information taken from SAS Institute's Web site, http://www.sasinstitute.com, February 2000.

5. Peter Drucker, speaking via teleconference at the 1998 Knowledge Forum at Haas School of Business, Berkeley, CA, as quoted by Don Cohen.

6. Bob Gett, "Face to Face with Bob Gett," interview by Don Cohen, *Knowledge Connections* 2, no. 1 (2000): 1.

7. See Robert Sutton and Andrew Hargadon, "Brainstorming Groups in Context: Effectiveness in a Product Design Firm," *Administrative Science Quarterly* 41 (1996): 683–718.

8. Quoted in Saidel and Cohen, "Collaboration at Russell Reynolds," 16.

9. Quoted in Frederick Reichheld, *The Loyalty Effect: The Hidden Force behind Growth, Profits, and Lasting Value* (Boston: Harvard Business School Press, 1996), 106.

10. Richard Sennett, *The Corrosion of Character: The Personal Consequences of Work in the New Capitalism* (New York: Norton, 1998), 24–25.

11. Cited by Tom Demarco in "Human Capital, Unmasked," *New York Times*, 14 April 1996, B1.

12. Reichheld, *The Loyalty Effect*, 91.

13. Don Cohen, unpublished case study written for Boston Financial, 1997.

14. Ghoshal and Bartlett, *The Individualized Corporation*.

15. Rousseau, *Psychological Contracts in Organizations*.

16. Ibid.

17. Ibid., 121, 128.

18. Packard, *The HP Way*, 133.

19. Sonnenfeld and Lazo, "United Parcel Service (A)," 13.

20. Ken Parks, UPS, phone interview by author (Cohen), 9 March 1999.

21. Dan McMackin, UPS, phone interview with author (Cohen), 1 March 1999.

22. See Ghoshal and Bartlett, *The Individualized Corporation*, 289.

23. Information about the ERI survey is based on Paul Siemion, conversation with author (Cohen), 1 June 1999, sample surveys, and results provided by UPS.

24. Sue Klepac, "Innovation Masters: Harnessing the Power of Individuals to Change a Culture," *Knowledge Directions* 2, no. 1 (Spring 2000): 22–32.

CHAPTER 7

1. Marshall MacLuhan and Quentin Fiore, *The Medium Is the Message* (New York: Bantam Books, 1967), 16, 67.

2. Tim Berners-Lee, *Weaving the Web: The Original Design and Ultimate Destiny of the World Wide Web by Its Inventor* (San Francisco: Harper, 1999), 206.

3. E. M. Forster, *The Machine Stops and Other Stories* (New York: Alfred A. Knopf, 1953).

4. Ithiel De Sola Pool, ed., *The Social Impact of the Telephone* (Cambridge, MA: MIT Press, 1977).

5. Neil Postman, *Building a Bridge to the Eighteenth Century* (New York: Alfred A. Knopf, 1999), 53.

6. Howard Rheingold, *The Virtual Community: Homesteading on the Electronic Frontier* (Reading, MA: Addison-Wesley, 1993).

7. Mathew Purdy, "Don't Know Online Talk? cu latr," *New York Times*, 26 January 2000.

8. Wanda Orlikowski, "Talking with Wanda Orlikowski," interview by Don Cohen, *Groundwork* (newsletter of the Ernst & Young Center for Business Innovation) 1, no. 2 (December 1996).

9. Diane Vaughan, *The Challenger Launch Decision: Risky Technology, Culture, and Deviance at NASA* (Chicago: University of Chicago Press, 1996).

10. Ibid., 357.

11. Ibid., 377.

12. Mulgan, *Connexity*, 28.

13. Michael Eisner, "Common Sense and Conflict," interview by Suzy Wetlaufer, *Harvard Business Review* 78, no. 1 (January–February 2000): 122.

14. These examples come from Brown and Duguid, *The Social Life of Information*, 67.

15. Wenger, *Communities of Practice*.

16. Brown and Duguid, *The Social Life of Information*, 68.

17. Thomas H. Davenport and Keri Pearlson, "Two Cheers for the Virtual Office," *Sloan Management Review* 39, no. 4 (Summer 1998): 56.

18. From a presentation by Tom Boyle, a knowledge management consultant, at the Institute for Knowledge Management Member Forum, Nice, France, September 1999.

19. Berners-Lee, *Weaving the Web*, 125.

20. Varian spoke at the Berkeley Knowledge Forum, Berkeley, California, September 1997.

21. Michael Burtha, conversations with author (Prusak), 1998 and 1999.

22. Tim Kinnel, "Making Large Collaborations Work: Solutions from High-Energy Physics," *Knowledge Directions* 1, no. 2 (Spring 1999): 20.

23. Ibid.

24. Charles Leadbeater, *Living on Thin Air* (London: Viking, 1999), 135–136.

25. Mulgan, *Connexity*, 28.

26. Lisa Guernsey, "Linking Classrooms, a World Apart, via the Internet," *New York Times*, 30 December 1999, B1.

Epilogue

1. Peter J. Howe, "Internet Boosters Singing the Blues," *The Boston Globe*, 1 June 2000, C1.
2. Quoted in Alex Berenson, "In Silicon Valley, Loyalty Means Paying a High Price," *New York Times*, 28 May 2000, 9.
3. Peter Drucker, speaking via teleconference at the 1998 Knowledge Forum at Haas School of Business, Berkeley, CA, as quoted by Don Cohen.

INDEX

❖

ABOUT THE AUTHORS

DON COHEN is a writer and editor who also spent seven years as Technology Manager of the school division of D.C. Heath, an educational publisher. His articles on knowledge management initiatives and ideas have been published in *California Management Review*, *Knowledge and Process Management*, and by The Conference Board. He created and edited *Groundwork*, the newsletter of the knowledge management program at the Ernst & Young Center for Business Innovation. He is currently Editor of *Knowledge Directions*, the journal of the IBM Institute for Knowledge Management, and the IKM's *Knowledge Connections* newsletter. Also a playwright and fiction writer, Cohen lives in Lexington, Massachusetts, with his wife Helen and their two daughters, Rebecca and Sarah.

LAURENCE PRUSAK is the Executive Director of the IBM Institute for Knowledge Management in Cambridge, Massachusetts. He has extensive consulting experience, within the U.S. and internationally, in helping firms leverage and optimize their information and knowledge resources. He has formerly been a management consultant and researcher at Ernst & Young and at Mercer Management Consulting. His professional background also includes work as a researcher and librarian at Baker Library at the Harvard Graduate School of Business Administration, and as a teacher of social and economic history at several universities. A respected authority in his field, Larry has lectured and been published widely. His books include *Managing Information Strategically* (coauthored with James McGee) and *Information Ecology* and *Working Knowledge* (both coauthored with Thomas Davenport). His awards include the SLA Professional Award for Contributions to the Field of Information Science, the H. W. Wilson Award for the year's best article on information science, and the Lewin Award from *Organization Science*.